Flight of the Pussywillow

My Continuing Life With T. Lobsang Rampa

Mama San Ra'ab Rampa

The Flight Of The Pussywillow
My Continuing Life With T. Lobsang Rampa

by

Mama San Ra'ab Rampa

ISBN-10: 1606110071

ISBN-13: 978-1606110072

Timothy Green Beckley: Editorial Director
Carol Rodriguez: Publisher's Assistant
Associate Editors: Sean Casteel & Tim Swartz
Special Thanks: William Kern

For Free Subscription To The Conspiracy Journal Write:
Tim Beckley/Global Communications-Inner Light
Box 753, New Brunswick, NJ 08903
Sign Up On Line: MRUFO8@hotmail.com
www.ConspiracyJournal.Com
www.TeslasSecretLab.Com

DECLARATION OF MRS. TUESDAY LOBSANG RAMPA

Lobsang Rampa knows the truth. He knows what he believes in and he is the person he claims to be. When the changeover occurred we had a very beautiful tabby cat with a silver coat and his attitude was surprising. Our tabby cat had extraordinary reactions towards the one I could call the New One. He showed an unusual respect towards him and anyone who saw him would have been most impressed by the wisdom of one of these 'dumb animals'.

As far as I know there is only one way to evaluate the declarations of my husband. It consists of reading all his books from the beginning to end. That's where the truth is. I am a registered Nurse and as such have a lot of experience concerning the observations of people, their attitudes, reactions or changes. Therefore I declare that everything Rampa has said is true, as far as I know. One of the most unpleasant things is the fierce hatred felt by some of the press. Yet those who react so harshly have declared publicly that they had read none of the books. Didn't a critic recently assert he had read one or two pages but did not want to continue reading it? Surprisingly, he began a fierce attack against a book he hadn't read! How, under those conditions can you 'reveal' anything to one whose mind is so closed? When a person doesn't want to believe, no proof in the world, or beyond this world would convince him. The belief has to come from the person himself.

One thing is clear, several persons have without respite attempted to get rid of Lobsang Rampa and to prevent him from writing. They haven't succeeded and they never will. As far as I know, Lobsang Rampa never was a plumber, and he is not today either...

When 'The Third Eye was published I made a declaration to the press. It was completely distorted. The press twisted my words and succeeded in making me claim that Rampa was an impostor. It is false, I have never thought nor claimed that he was an impostor. On the contrary, I assert, as I've always said that his books are true...

I am my husband's wife, and when a woman is married to a man, she understands him, his moods, his peculiarities. If, suddenly, everything changes in him, if it becomes evident to the woman that she lives with another man, a really different man, we have to accept the reality of the way it is. It can't be proved. I was in this situation. I saw a change occurring, I observed how the transmigration happened. However, I continued to live with him. But everything is different. We live rather like brother and sister, both making the best of the difficult situation we are in. But as I've witnessed all theses things, as I've experienced it, there remains no doubt it is the truth.

A Thought

Yesterday was once today

and Tomorrow soon will be.

Today is all that matters!

PUSSY WILLOW

SATO? What's That?

Well, a book has to have a title, eh? So how about a 'computer code' version of what this is all about? It is...

Sindhi — And — The — Others.

I love cats, any cats; small cats, big cats, thin cats, fat cats, skinny cats, toms and queens, kittens and adults. Cats. ANY cats.

The Lady Ku'ei, one of my Cat Children, was very fond of remarking to the Guv, 'My Ma will stop and chat with any old tom cat she may happen to meet up with', but she did not disapprove for Miss Ku'ei was no snob.

No doubt this little volume will receive its share of criticism but that is no cause for concern . . . it is written for my friends, those people who have expressed an interest in the Guv's Family. I am reminded of a quotation by the Guv and, since it is heartily endorsed by me, I will use it here:

'Dogs bark, but the caravan moves on . . . ,

'Critics usually are those without the wits to write a good book.'

FLIGHT OF THE PUSSYWILLOW

CHAPTER ONE

SINDHI is a cat, a Siamese cat, and although she is not living on the earth now she is very much alive elsewhere. It was one of the more positive acts of my life that I cared for this little person during the very short time she was with us.

We had been in Canada a little over one year when we met her, and she had a most charming way of getting around one, of getting her own way. At her best she was most affectionate, tucking her small head under my chin as I held her, telling me in cat language that she loved me.

How did I find myself with a third cat person when there were two Siamese people already quite well established in the household? Well, really I had little choice in the matter because a man who was employed in a pet shop asked if a home could be found for her. He had heard about Miss Ku'ei and Mrs. Fifi and he said he understood we were very fond of cats, especially Siamese, and that we understood them. He had a feeling that Sindhi was not happy and would we please go and see her at his home where we could find his wife, and talk to her. Since I have mentioned Ku'ei and Fifi, and if you have read 'Living with the Lama', it will be apparent who 'we' are. I am 'Ma' to cats, and I am proud of the fact that Mrs. Greywhiskers paid me the great honor of dedicating her book to me. The other one of 'us' is the 'Guv' to cats, and he was kind enough to translate the contents of 'Living with the Lama' from cat language into words which could be understood by humans. Since cats make pictures instead of words this must have entailed quite a bit of ingenuity on the part of the Guv, and a good amount of cooperation from Fifi.

At that time we had a fairly big car, a used one, otherwise we would not have been driving around in a color combination of pink and gold. It was rather like a woman wearing a pink or a vivid red outfit — in a few days she would be recognized a mile away. Each time we took out our pink Mercury we could imagine everybody in the neighborhood shrieking 'Here they come! With their cat an' all!' It was the very same automobile which nearly scared the daylights out of Miss Ku'ei and me when the steering "went" one day while we sped along the Tecumseh road towards Windsor. Ku'ei was definitely the motoring type and whenever possible she went with us, either shopping or sight-seeing, even when we collected the mail from the post office at Walkerville, near Windsor; hence the remarks 'here they come with their cat!'

As we drove along to the pet shop man's home I wondered what Ku'ei was thinking about it all, but then I decided 'sufficient unto the day—' Eventually we found the house and the Guv stayed in the car while I went to the door and rang the bell while just at that moment Mrs. Pet shop Man appeared in the entrance. As I discussed with her the reason for our visit she seemed most relieved and told me that her nerves were bad; the cat was getting her down and she doubted if she could stand it any longer. A wailing noise was coming from someplace inside, a voice which could only be that of a Siamese, and then Sindhi appeared. A poor thin little creature looking so pathetic, and no wonder, for the woman had no doubt transmitted her nervous state to the tiny bundle of fur standing there. 'What can you do about it?' the woman queried of us; 'I doubt if I could stand it another night,' she continued. 'Can't you take her and find her a home?'

By this time the Guv had approached and was taking control of the situation. He could see she was neurotic (a very thin discontented individual) and she was imploring us to take the cat, the cat who was so obviously very miserable.

What COULD WE DO? We had two mature Lady cats at home who were getting along quite well together, so what was going to happen if we came home with Sindhi? Quickly we decided, and as soon as we had bundled ourselves into the auto and Mrs. Pet shop had waved her gratitude, Sindhi, who must have been about one year old, let out the most piercing yowl. She told the world in general that she must have a tom; so here we were, faced with another dilemma. While she was in this condition it was impossible to take her home to our apartment so we thought we had better make a detour and call at the office of our friend, Mr. L. the veterinarian, hoping we would find him there. He had treated Fifi and Ku'ei when the humidity of Windsor had caused discomfort in their ears, and Ku'ei had had eye trouble also, necessitating the removal of the inner eyelid which was beginning to enlarge and soon would have covered the entire eye. This was a phenomenon peculiar to the Windsor area and, in our opinion, caused through excessive spraying of insecticide all around the side streets where there were trees and bushes, and which had been carried in the air on to the plants and grass of our garden. The little cat nestled close to me as we drove along, quiet for a while; then came another piercing shriek, 'I want a tom, I must have a tom!' Poor little girl cat; we found she had sight in only one eye and we commented that she looked like Egyptian Nefertiti as she also had one blind eye. Anyway, we took to the little creature and we told her that soon she would be living with us; soon she would be sharing our home.

Mr. L. was a charming person, one of the nicest veterinarians we have met, and we have come across quite a number in our travels around Canada. He had a cat too, a Siamese tom, so he was very interested in our Cat family.

The first time he visited us, when we lived near Tecumseh, he arrived at the front door one evening where I met him and took him into the living room where Ku'ei and Fifi were awaiting his arrival. When he saw them he uttered a delightful greeting, 'Aren't they just living dolls', and we always remember that first meeting, while many times we have used that selfsame expression in referring to certain felines.

Well, fortunately Dr. L. was in his office when we arrived and, after taking a look at her, decided Sindhi should be left with him and she would be spayed that very day.

Fortunately it was the beginning of the day so we left her and arranged to come back and collect her in the evening, assuming her condition was satisfactory by the evening. It seemed a rather different procedure from England, where a cat would be left at the Pet Hospital for two nights (the night previous and the night following the operation), in the case of a female being spayed. A tom, by comparison, was treated rather differently; his neutering operation, not being so serious, could be done 'while you wait' type of thing. However, I took a little tom cat to the veterinarian here in Calgary the other day, and his treatment was the reverse of our previous experiences in this country. Smokey, an all-over black cat, was our neighbor, and his so-called Mistress (who was really his servant) was sick and therefore unable to take him, so I volunteered. Smokey was to be kept for two nights, as though he were a female, and it is interesting to see how customs change, but the Westside Pet Hospital is a most pleasant place where our own two felines are treated with the utmost politeness and care by the doctors and staff. I have often thought that so-called animals are treated with greater care and respect by the 'animal doctor' than are many human animals who are left to the mercy of certain medicos.

Wherever we have lived it has been one of my earliest and most pleasant duties to find a veterinarian, have our Cat People meet him, and it has always paid off. The Cat is checked over and, in the event she needs treatment at a later date, well, she is not afraid because she has already been introduced and (we hope) feels friendly towards her doctor; therefore she knows what to expect. 'A crazy idea' someone says, but is it really so strange? Considering a plant can wither and die if approached by someone who is unsympathetic (I have seen this happen quite recently in the case of a sensitive plant), isn't it just as important, if not more so, for your pet to be prepared in advance against the time he or she may have need of professional services?

But to return to Windsor and to the events of almost a decade and a half ago when we thanked our lucky stars that we had such a wonderful ally in Dr. L. We returned home to our apartment contented in the knowledge that Sindhi was receiving expert attention, and with the assurance that we would receive a telephone call; so now our thoughts turned to the Cat Persons left at home, Miss Ku'ei and Mrs Fifi.

Naturally those two were eagerly waiting for the latest developments, though they were so highly telepathic that we had little explaining to do. Often the Guv had said he always knew when I would be returning if I had been out shopping, or out on business, or something. He would know at least five minutes before my return because Miss Ku'ei would stretch, rise from her chair, walk around a bit, and then sit by the door to wait for her Ma. When I made a short visit to Canada, before we finally moved here from Ireland, I wore a locket around my neck in which a clipping of Ku'ei's fur was encased. This enabled her to keep in closer contact with me telepathically, thus helping the Guv to know how I was faring on the other side of the Atlantic. We could tell by their manner that Ku and Feef half expected us to walk in accompanied by some strange, unknown creature who they would have to tolerate and teach. They sniffed around us, did some thinking, and decided the best thing to do would be to 'wait and see' and, if the worst should happen, well then, true to their nature they would make the best of the situation. The day wore on; we waited anxiously by the telephone, and around four o'clock came the welcome voice of Mr. L. The operation had been successful, he told us; the patient was resting as comfortably as could be expected, having not long recovered from the anesthetic, and it would be alright if we came around any time after five to collect her. So, after five we drove off, getting caught in the rush hour traffic, but at last we reached the Pet Hospital.

Sindhi looked wan and rather the worse for wear as she was passed to me; and I placed a rug around her since Windsor was quite chilly in March, then we went out to the car, after being instructed to see that she did not tear her stitches out, as another little girl cat did some years later. It was a little after six o'clock when we arrived home and I took the bundle of fur to my own room because we thought it better to be on the safe side at first — the result could have been unfortunate if she had been left with the others in her weakened condition, and different surroundings. She took a little fluid nourishment and I was very encouraged to notice she seemed to show quite a liking for me. Later in the evening we were to have a showing of photographic slides, in color.

We had a nice projector and a big screen, and we were to view these (our latest) color pictures. . . . The Guv, you see, is a superb photographer (he was actually complimented by Kodak upon his beautiful pictures) and these were his latest flower pictures, mostly close-ups, appearing much larger- than-life in their effect. These many years later I can remember vividly the glorious reproductions, looking almost too perfect to be the real thing. That is something else about the Guv, whatever he touches immediately becomes ALIVE, never mind whether it be an automobile, a radio, or a camera. It gives me great joy to be able to write about some of the things which he has done, things which made a deep impression upon me but which are so ordinary to him that he would not think there was anything unusual in what he was doing. In some of these transparencies, closeups of flowers, which at that time were providing us with great interest and which we found most educational, there was an atmosphere of the ethereal, and without actually being there and seeing for yourself it would be difficult to believe how many faces and little fairy-like figures were portrayed within these various hued petals. Fairies! Nature spirits! A figment of the imagination? Whatever they were they fitted the accepted idea of how fairies and nature spirits would appear, those little people who tend the growth of plants and flowers, and who are frequently observed by clairvoyants. During the filming I had to hold Sindhi on my lap, with a little rug underneath her, for she still felt rather unsure in the different surroundings and we wanted to show her quite clearly that she really was wanted. Ku'ei and Fifi were 'somewhere', receiving impressions, because they could know exactly what was going on without actually watching the screen. Sindhi was snoozing and completely relaxed in the knowledge that at last she was home and wanted. One thing which seemed to interest her was the tall person who was helping with the projector; the tall person with golden hair, the blue eyes and the graceful movements.

Probably she considered she and the tall person were nearer the same age than either of them were with the other members of the Family. If she had not already done so she would soon find out that it was permissible to refer to the blue-eyed, golden haired person as 'Buttercup', and that it was in order to address her thus. Mrs. Greywhiskers, Fifi, had been responsible for this name; she had considered it to be most appropriate and, as everyone in the family approved, it had come to be generally accepted. If you have read Fifi's book, 'Living with the Lama', by T. Lobsang Rampa, you will have learned a good deal about Buttercup and her activities. . . . Oh, yes, Sindhi would be briefed as to how she was expected to behave, and told what humans expected of her because Fifi, with Ku'ei's approval, was very orderly. She believed in firm discipline, coupled with kindness and compassion (the latter was something she had missed for the whole of her life until she came to us about two years previously), and she always tried to avoid causing unnecessary work for those who looked after her needs, these persons being Buttercup and myself. In those two years that she had lived with us we were accepted as her Real Family, and ours was her True Home. Being without sight it was fortunate that Miss Ku'ei enjoyed guiding her around the rooms until Fifi had become familiarized with all the objects such as tables, chairs, and other furniture which might be hazardous to a blind, elderly cat person. Now we would have to see how we would all manage with a sightless woman cat and a half-sighted girl cat.

What a responsibility for the Lady Ku'ei!

CHAPTER TWO

'I THINK it's about time we moved away from here,' announced the Guv when he came home one afternoon, soon after Sindhi's arrival. 'For heaven's sake,' I answered, 'we haven't been here very long, and anyhow where were you thinking of moving to?' We talked it over and decided we didn't have much choice in the matter since we were being troubled by press reporters, and we were gradually losing the privacy we had looked for when we came to Canada. It was only a little over twelve months since we arrived in the Windsor area and at first it had been quite enjoyable. We had lived for a few months in a furnished house near Tecumseh, on the edge of Lake St. Clair, and during that period we were left in peace. All that bothered us was the extreme cold as we had arrived in midwinter, an extremely severe winter it turned out to be too. The day after we arrived we walked down to the frozen lake, taking Miss Ku'ei, wrapped in a rug; but we had to hurry home because we had not become acclimatized to the change from Ireland, where it was never too 'freezing' by the salt water of the Irish sea, which we had just left. We found it almost impossible to go out walking at all, even to the store a little way down the road — a little store by the name of Stop'n Shop. Poor Buttercup spent a few of the most miserable weeks of her life feeling perpetually chilled, so we decided to be sensible and stay in, or use the second-hand car which we purchased soon after our arrival. It was impossible to manage without an automobile because in that area, in those days, there were no deliveries of supplies and we needed to make daily trips to the post office. By the time we moved to the Windsor district, some miles from our previous home, winter had passed and we enjoyed the warm April days; and there was an added attraction when the lakers and seagoing vessels started moving along the Detroit river, a sight which provided much interest and enjoyment.

FLIGHT OF THE PUSSYWILLOW

It was quite exciting to have the Queen pass right in front of our house, too, following the opening of the St. Lawrence Seaway. She was on the way to Chicago and we had a wonderful view from our balcony, and the Guv took some interesting pictures through a tele- scope, one of a helicopter which hovered overhead, and the effect was just as though you were stand- ing right beside the craft. The Queen might have been paying us a personal visit, everything seemed so close. We took many pictures in those days, and it was simple when one had a car for we could tour around looking for pictorial scenes. I used to have a 35 mm. camera but since we do not travel around very much these days my interest in photography has suffered. I remember taking some wintry scenes across the Detroit river, when it was covered with ice, and when the slides were shown they looked quite artistic — the frozen river, the leafless trees, and the Detroit skyline in the back- ground.

So, by the time spring 1960 came around we had spent about one year in that particular house. It was a convenient location in many ways, especially for shopping and post office facilities. We had garage space for which we were grateful considering the severe winters we had to endure. Apart from reporters coming around, life was quite pleasant. Since we were 'New Ca- nadians' and were not used to the ways of 'Old Canadians' there was one incident which ruffled us somewhat. It was our first Halloween in this coun- try and on the following morning we noticed the garden gate was missing. When we telephoned the police to report the incident we were somewhat surprised to be told, 'you should be thankful you didn't lose the roof'. There must be something very harmonious in the particular area where we lived for, on many mornings, around five o'clock and before the heavy traffic came along to assault our ears, one could hear very pleasant music — apparently coming from the river. It was most interesting and we enjoyed it immensely. Another unusual phenomenon to recollect, and I will not be alarmed if some- one should label me 'screwy' or of too vivid an imagination, but this was a very interesting sight. At certain times there could be seen shadowy fig- ures, tall figures, moving about in front of the Detroit skyscrapers, but nearer the river. I often wondered about them and then I ventured to mention the matter to the Guv who sees many things which escape the senses of most of us. He merely remarked, 'Well, what of it, it is merely people going about their business in another dimension.' Well, after a reporter had waylaid the Guv while he was taking a leisurely drive by the river, telling the Guv: 'I know who you are and I am going to write an article about you for the local news- paper', we knew that there would be little peace left for us in that location. The Guv was right when he came home and told us, 'It is time we moved away from here.' The problem was, where to go? 'How about Vancouver?' someone said, and it sounded good. Certainly the climate should be more suitable for us, and we had been told that Vancouver Island was very much like England except it was warmer and there was less rain than in England. But how could we take a chance and move unless someone could go first, just for a visit, to see if it really was the place for us! After some discussion the Guv said he would go himself because it was easier for him to do that than take charge of three Siamese lady cats. Also, he knew I did not enjoy traveling, and he always got a bit worried on the few occasions I had to be away. Sometimes, he says, just at the moment when I should be watching for traffic, my mind wanders, making it a full- time job keeping a mental check on me. Well, Buttercup kindly offered to go along because she does not mind traveling, and she knew someone should be with the Guv for even in those days his health was very poor.

All of our mental processes were stepped up into high gear because making the arrangements and getting everything ready would be a joint effort. This was going to be quite a journey as far as our little Family was concerned because we did not enjoy being separated at any time, never mind this long journey over so many miles. Even if planes do these flights in just a few hours from one continent to another, and the whole length of our own continent, it is still a considerable distance, and if you are not used to traveling, well it can be a little worrying wondering if all will be well. So the air tickets were obtained, suitcases were packed, and the travelers departed; and I remember it was just one week before Easter.

Fifi and Ku'ei must have had many discussions about their responsibilities during the week ahead for this mission could not be accomplished satisfactorily in less than perhaps five days. There would be no sense in turning round immediately on arrival and heading home too quickly; that would accomplish nothing. Of course the three hours difference in time was an advantage. At any rate, these two veteran cats must have decided between them that they would be able to deal with the situation since it couldn't be any worse than the period a few months earlier when they had a MONKEY to cope with. That had certainly been an experience for the whole Family. At first we felt a bit lonesome when all at once we realized the others had left, but then we decided we had better get on with the process of day-to-day living. It was a good feeling, very satisfying to have these three creatures entrusted to my care for a few days. At the same time it was not without a slight feeling of apprehension because it was the first time I had stayed alone since the advent of the 'littlest cat' as we sometimes referred to Sindhi. It had been simple in the case of Fifi and Ku'ei only; we had always survived without any major incidents for short periods, but they always preferred to have the Guv around as much as possible.

Things had not progressed too smoothly during the past few weeks, and during that time we had to experiment a little. For almost two years Fifi and Ku'ei had lived together amicably, even if Ku'ei had been known to mutter occasionally (in fun of course), 'I wonder if I was wise in having that old biddy to live with me; after all it does take away some of the attention from me.' For a Siamese that was probably quite a natural way of viewing things for they thrive on adulation and they couldn't survive without constant loving care and a sincere and definite interest in their well-being. Very recently I heard of someone in this city who had a pair of these creatures and, unfortunately, she was obliged to go out to earn a living. Due to the lack of attention this person was able to provide in that they had to stay alone for periods much too long, she lost first one of her pets and soon afterwards the other one passed on. To some extent all cats suffer through being left too long by their so-called owners; they cannot stand appearing to be neglected, and this is especially true of the Siamese.

Sindhi needed and demanded attention, and being much younger than the others (barely more than a kitten) she wanted more ACTION and fun and this gave us cause for concern. While Miss Ku could easily skip out of the way, it was more difficult for Fifi who was not able to see which way to go to avoid the Baby Cat; but Sindhi, too, with sight in only one eye must have had her problems in direction finding. One just needs to put one's hand over one eye to realize how difficult monocular sight can be, how severely handicapped one is in gauging movements and judging distances.

CHAPTER THREE

It was obvious that Fifi and Ku'ei were becoming nervous, never knowing if they would be left in peace for awhile, and therefore the whole matter
had to be given serious consideration. First of all we allowed Sindhi to go to
someone else; but this was not satisfactory so she had to return to my care.
She had quite definitely adopted me, and so the Sindhi problem became
my responsibility. During the daytime it was not too difficult since we had a
sunroom, with a door, where the Baby Cat spent a good deal of time sleeping and sunning herself. As she washed herself, and the sun's rays fell on
her fur, she was able to provide herself with a good supply of vitamins. It
was a nice pleasant room, the same room Mr. Monkey had occupied, but in
the summer months it was almost too pleasant in that it faced south and the
temperature could become quite uncomfortable by midday and in the afternoons. At night, as bedtime approached, it was a rather different situation: Fifi and Ku'ei had been accustomed to spending the nights each in their
own chair by the side of my bed, with Ku'ei spending long periods right
beside me, on the bed. My bedroom door would be left open and they would
wander in and out at will, for cats enjoy nocturnal wanderings as everybody
knows. Ku'ei had always been MY cat, while Fifi had taken on the responsibility of the Guv's welfare, but now that we had Sindhi she seemed to need
my wholehearted attention, with no interference from the others. She felt so
insecure (as could be expected considering her early-life experiences), and
she wondered (all the time being afraid) whether her new position as my
'Baby' was in jeopardy. She considered that her place was by me, on the
bed, and that there should be no competition from anyone, cat or human,
especially cat. This was a very difficult situation, particularly for the one who
had been so close to me for around seven or eight years, and it was to her
everlasting credit that Miss Ku'ei handled the situation superbly, giving way
to Sindhi continually. Ku'ei's life had not been an easy one; she had shared

our many adversities, and comforted us in our moments of sadness. As a kitten she had had a sister (Su Wei) who lived for only a few months, a victim of the dreaded disease 'feline gastro-enteritis'.

After that sad episode we became closer in our understanding of each other; and it was a moment of great joy when she found another companion in Mrs. Fifi a few years later. By the time Sindhi came on the scene the others had been together about two years. The name Ku'ei signifies 'in memory of the one who went before'; and she had come to me at a time when I was suffering from the loss of a beautiful silver tabby who, at age eleven, succumbed to an attack of pneumonia. The Guv had named Miss Ku'ei and it suited her very well. It was such a suitable and, I thought, 'delightful' name, and it has been used by many other felines who desired to be named after her.

Altogether I owe a great deal to Cat People in general, and especially to those who have been my companions, both in my sad and happy moments. When I would take a bath in the evenings I was full of apprehension lest a fight develop (or at least a fierce argument) while I, the sergeant major to cats, was otherwise occupied. I solved the problem by taking Sindhi to the bathroom with me, and it turned out to be a beautiful idea for we had a lot of fun. First she would sit on the edge of the bath watching me, and when I had finished and the nice hot water had flowed away, Sindhi would hop into the empty bathtub and roll around enjoying the warmth and the smoothness of the tub. In the end it was a problem to get her to come out of the bathroom. When Ku'ei was a kitten she had enjoyed waiting for me while I took my bath; but she had never gone further than the edge of the tub.

After a day had passed there was a telephone call from Vancouver to let us know the other part of the Family had reached their destination and that they were eager to know how we at home were faring. On the few occasions the Guv has been away from home he has always tried to talk to me directly, but he has great difficulty since it causes him much strain to 'tune in' to the mechanical device and decipher what the other person is saying over the phone. Anyone who has visited him has expressed great surprise that he could understand what they were saying since they were given to understand he is quite deaf, and then it would be explained that he uses lip reading a great deal, otherwise it would be too difficult to carry on a conversation. Once he has become familiar with a person's wavelength, when the person visualizes their message, as well as speaking the words, then he can deal with the telephone. On this particular occasion the line was clear, so after a greeting from Buttercup we heard the Guv saying, 'Hello Ra-ab, how are you and the cat children?' All the little people had gathered around me silently, sensing the Guv was not too far away after all, when they could hear his voice. As he inquired about each one separately the ears would fluctuate so that she might enjoy the greeting to the full. Whenever he was away he always made a point of inquiring about everyone and everything because he wanted to know exactly what was happening so that he might keep a mental check on the situation. He always told me never to hesitate in letting him know if I should run into a problem, never mind whether it would be in the middle of the night, whenever he was away from home. He told us there had not been time to tour the various districts of Vancouver but we would be given all details when they returned at the end of the week. The cats settled down after we had said goodbye, and commenced washing themselves in preparation for a long discussion about Vancouver and the Guv. I understand that cats believe in the maxim, 'When in doubt, start washing'. The Guv says they indulge in serious conversation while appearing to be merely engaged in a routine toilet operation.

It was surprising how the time passed by, and soon we were preparing for the traveler's return. We had done a little reading, listened to the radio, and had our moments of fun playing with plastic balls, ping pong balls, and chasing a long piece of string. Our little radio (a plastic one) was molded in the shape of a handbag, and we listened to stations from Detroit, as well as from Windsor. We could have the stations fairly loud since we would not be disturbing anyone, and I always marveled at the speed with which the Detroit announcers and news readers spilled out the words. I can usually follow a rapid speaker, but these boys were the fastest talkers I had ever heard. At night in our room we kept the volume down when everyone was home, but it was rather a strain, especially when we wanted to listen to music, and they did have good concerts from Detroit. When I had mentioned to the Guv that I wished there was provision for private listening, it was no sooner said than done. The necessary parts were obtained and presto — we had a plug and socket all fixed up. After that there was no limit to the volume, unless we reached the point of distortion when, of course, we turned it down. I did the turning down, the tuning and changing of stations, even though Sindhi might well have done it for me, for she did some interesting things. We had a carriage clock and she had a habit of reaching up to the shelf where it stood, and she would touch the repeater button because she enjoyed hearing the

FLIGHT OF THE PUSSYWILLOW

clock striking. No doubt she would have found the radio controls a little more difficult to operate. Until that time I did not know that if I left the private listening device plugged in to the radio it would run down my batteries, whether the radio was switched on or not. Since I was told about it I have always taken out the plug after switching off the radio.

Something else I learned was that unused batteries, that is new batteries, should be kept side-by-side, and the exposed metal parts should not be allowed to come together and make contact, otherwise they would run themselves down. This cannot possibly be well-known considering the number of times a store has handed me a package of batteries all jumbled together. Sometimes I have wished I knew something of basic electronics, but at least am now able to test my own batteries with a small device given to me by the Guv. It is a handy little instrument and I feel quite important when I am asked to test the batteries for someone else's radio.

But to return to my responsibilities of caring for the home and my trio of felines. At that time we had a neighbor who was living temporarily in the lower part of the house, and on the few occasions when she, or we, needed a little change, she would come up and chat with me while we took a cup of tea together. The cats enjoyed having an occasional visitor and she was an interesting person, an avid photographer, and very interested in oil painting. Her name was artistic sounding too — she was called 'Flora', and she was a small person physically. Although I had a very good idea of the needs of my Cat children, I still could not communicate with them as clearly as with another human; so I enjoyed this little diversion which left me feeling refreshed. On occasion though I may have remarked that one of the cats may be needing something, and the Guv has replied, 'Well that is exactly what she is saying.' Fortunately there were two nice people living in the house next to ours: two sisters, who were teachers, and their Family had been amongst the early settlers in Canada (they had emigrated from France). They owned their house, and ours also, and I could always call upon them in an emergency. They had another home in Amherstburg, a beautiful cottage, which they had built some years earlier, and they loved to spend their summer vacations in that cottage in Amherstburg. Although we did not see much of them we did meet occasionally in the garage, which we shared, where we chatted for awhile. But being teachers they were away most of the day, and often on weekends they took off for the cottage. Sometimes they would take a peek over the dividing wall of our gardens and they would admire

FLIGHT OF THE PUSSYWILLOW

Ku'ei and Fifi who loved to sit on the grass down there, and eat some of it if they were in the mood.

Fifi took some watching in those days for she would walk around and out through the garden gate, not realizing she was 'out of bounds'; or perhaps she wanted to have some fun with me. As soon as I found she was missing I hurried along the alleyway to get her and bring her back into the garden.

For an elderly lady cat she certainly did move quickly; but we had a happy time that first summer on Riverside Drive.

Now it was the spring of another year and we were feeling very happy in the knowledge that soon our Family would all be together again. With the best will and the greatest effort we all became just a little bored. The Cat people liked to have the Family around, being busy, thus giving themselves an interest in following our activities. So, on the Friday, which happened to be Good Friday (towards the end of April), we had a big family reunion when the others returned. We talked about Vancouver, which seemed a nice enough place, and the Guv wanted to know all about how we had managed at home; and he spoke to each Cat person separately. Unfortunately Buttercup felt sick when she arrived, but after having a rest she quickly recovered.

I received a very nice gift of a book entitled 'The Cat', which was written by a veterinarian. It was inscribed 'To the Ma of all the Cats' and, although the writing closely resembled the Guv's, it was 'from Sindhi Blue Eyes'. It is still one of my greatest treasures and whenever I take it from the bookshelf I feel that Sindhi is close by.

CHAPTER FOUR

So life continued on with many things just the same as ever, and we found that to live one day at a time was the best way to survive; but we had to make a few adjustments it seemed. Previously Miss Ku'ei had always accompanied the Guv and me when we took the car to collect the mail each morning, except on the high humidity, hot stifling days when even she couldn't enjoy it and would stay at home with Fifi. Now we realized we could not leave Sindhi alone with Fifi because we could not be sure that the little cat would not harass Fifi — and that we would not tolerate. The only thing to do then was to leave Miss Ku'ei with Mrs. Fifi for company, and take the Baby Cat with us. Fifi did not enjoy traveling since her life had been too full of it, but for Ku'ei it would be quite a sacrifice to forfeit her morning's drive. It had made her unhappy on those days when the humid heat proved too much for anyone who was unable to shed her fur coat, but Ku'ei was a most understanding person. Sindhi would sit in the car with the Guv while I went into the Walkerville Post Office to collect the mail, and then we would take her for a drive around the streets before returning home. The Guv used to say that if someone approached the car while they were waiting for me she would become quite fierce, telling them in colorful language what she thought of them. He was most concerned because an untrained Siamese can be quite frightening and he didn't know what to do about the situation. In this case there seemed to be more to it than simply an untrained Siamese since, when she was free of her 'attacks' she was the sweetest little person one could hope to meet. She was given every consideration and understanding, and the Guv never spared himself in trying to fathom the cause of her apparent unhappiness and unpredictability. We debated whether the difficulty could in some way be connected with her blindness of one eye. Was there some damage? And what had caused the eye problem anyway?

FLIGHT OF THE PUSSYWILLOW

There was no mistaking the fact that something was very wrong, and there was a definite need for constant supervision. Therefore, I continued to devote more and more time to her needs, and I tried to show her that being difficult did not help at all.

By this time the Guv had started to write another book, which meant controlling the Cat People more than ever, especially the little one. So, as I had to devote much time in the role of Cat Guard, I decided to put some of my thoughts and experiences down on paper. I brought out the typewriter and with a big feeling of hope and an idea of achieveing something, I decided that if my charges behaved themselves, and if there were not too many diversions, I might possibly end up with something in the way of an acceptable story. I made notes about the Guv; how we had been together for about thirteen years and how the number thirteen had cropped up so often, especially in the years since we had been associated with each other. And then it came to my mind about the Dalai Lama of Tibet, the 'Great Thirteenth' about whom I had read and heard so much.

He who was acknowledged to be the last Incarnation of the Dalai Lamas, the fourteenth having publicly proclaimed that he was not an incarnation. My story was going to be full of interesting things, to me at any rate, and hopefully to a few other people. I would have a lot to say about Ku'ei who had come to me in a time of great stress, and when just a few weeks old had sat on my shoulder while together we read a beautiful cat story called 'The Cat who went to Heaven'; a delightfully illustrated book all about a little cat who had such a happy experience that it was more than she could contain, and she went straight to Heaven. Unfortunately that book is most likely out of print now. If only I could get all my ideas organized and set out clearly in my mind, then I would be in business.

Some time earlier I had been given to understand that a publisher would be pleased to consider a manuscript if I gave it a 'fairly strong occult flavor'. However, it was not to be since I had not felt qualified to write upon the occult, though I was not without experiences in this direction, and the moment had passed.

When I had put together a few pages of notes my Cat Guard duties were less quiet because the Guv had finished his book, but I enjoyed the relaxation it provided for it was a long time since I had done any writing. For a change, and because I had the urge to do so, I had enjoyed a period of study-

17

ing handwriting instead of concentrating on writing myself. I found this to be a most fascinating science and I met some interesting people, in the business world and in private, and I saw some most interesting handwriting specimens. The other day we were talking about spontaneous impressions etcetera and the Guv said that if he was to alter something after the first writing it was never as good as his first effort. I remarked that a number of times I had written down passages as they had occurred to me, and experiences just as they had come into my head at odd moments, when I felt 'inspired', but that usually I just threw the pages away. I said I didn't see any use in keeping them for who would be interested in them anyway? Buttercup suggested it was foolish to destroy something you write for it is in those moments of inspiration that one captures something which, if not kept, could be lost forever. The Guv maintains that writing is perhaps one per cent inspiration and the remaining ninety-nine per cent perspiration — in other words, plain hard work. While the Guv had been writing his book, which was all planned in advance and just needed transmitting to paper, he was thinking of the future. Vancouver would have suited us he said, but how to get there! We would not be allowed to have the cats with us in the cabin if we traveled by air; or in the compartment if we contemplated a train journey; and it was too far by road. I have often wondered why one cannot take a cat, or any pet, in a private room on a train in Canada, even though one can do so in the United States. I have traveled from Canada to New York and from New York to Canada with one or two cats in an ordinary sleeping compartment, on an American train, without any trouble at all. Perhaps we Canadians are somewhat neurotic blaming cats for causing our hay fever, various allergies, and nervous disorders, when a good part of it is imagination — all in our heads. We have made many inquiries about these rules and were told by the authorities that at one time pets WERE allowed on Canadian trains, especially if one traveled in a private sitting room or bedroom. However, the public objected and the practice was discontinued. If it was within my power to have those rules changed I most certainly would, thus avoiding much discomfort and actual misery for many pets.

We were agreed upon one thing and that was to find another place to live; then someone thought of Fort Erie which was a rather convenient journey and not too far to travel. It would take about four hours by rail, with no changes. Once more it would mean someone going first to see what it was really like, this place situated at one end of the Niagara Parkway, close to the Peace Bridge, linking Canada to the United States. The Guv decided to take a look at the district and he said it would be quite suitable but decidedly smaller than Windsor, with a population of around nine thousand. It seemed to be a flourishing little community. We thought that a complete change might result in an improvement in Sindhi's attitude, and we sincerely hoped it would have this effect. The main problem was that Fort Erie, like many places, had an accommodation shortage and we were unable to find a house or an apartment. I was finding it more and more difficult to cope with the feline problem as, sometimes when I was alone with Sindhi in my room she would become excited and start to struggle in my arms. It seemed that whenever she became excited something beyond her control happened and she would become very difficult to handle. Often I had to leave her in the room alone, closing the door, and find myself another place to stay for the remainder of the night — often on the divan in the living room, with Ku'ei and Fifi.

We had arranged to have a Fort Erie newspaper sent to us so that we might follow the advertisements for accommodations because there were so very few vacancies that it was rarely they were ever referred to a real estate office. One day I was half-heartedly looking over the advertisement page when I noticed 'House for Rent or Sale', so my interest was aroused and it was only a matter of seconds before I was on the telephone to the advertiser, and soon I was in possession of the essential details. It seemed this dwelling was situated about three miles from Fort Erie and about sixteen miles from Niagara Falls, and set in its own grounds — part of which was reserved for summer cabins and holiday-makers.

It seemed to be just what we needed and the owner, Mrs. C., said there were lots of trees and she was sure the whole place would appeal to us. The house had been, and still was being used as an office from which Mrs. C ran the cabins; but the season would be over by the end of August and the house would be available at any time in September.

This meant another journey to view the premises, and another discussion as to who would go to see the place. I offered to make the journey this time, but I had to consider the 'Little Cat'. Since out neighbor, Flora, owned a car, and as she would have some time to spare on the weekend, I said 'How about me taking Sindhi along?'. Everyone appeared rather taken aback but I could not have gone away with a clear conscience if I had to leave her behind for I should have been worried to death wondering what she was up to.

FLIGHT OF THE PUSSYWILLOW

Some people can just take off, leaving behind all their problems, and they seem to be none the worse for it; but I have to stay home or take my problems with me. It is not that I think other people cannot manage, but if I decide to undertake a venture I have to see it through, and Sindhi was my 'venture'.

I left a note under Flora's door asking her to telephone me when she returned from the office so that I might approach her with my idea. Fortunately the proposal met with her approval. Actually, she said she would enjoy the outing she was sure, and so we went ahead with our plans. The Guv was somewhat concerned about Sindhi undertaking such a long journey, as I knew he would be, but it was obvious that either she would accompany me or I would not be able to go.

We planned the undertaking for the weekend since Flora had to be at the office during the week, so we arranged to start out on the Saturday and return on Sunday. We fitted the car out comfortably, and Sindhi would sit in the rear seat beside me with her traveling basket, a nice warm blanket, and a tray for her other needs of nature. Food was provided also because she would need that on arrival, if not before, since cats often will not take food while traveling.

Their metabolism seems to undergo a change and they do not seem to feel the need for anything until they reach their destination and after they have got themselves settled. Domestic cats take about three days to settle down, to get their bearings and become orientated; and until they do get settled they suffer, so that is a good reason for keeping a cat indoors for at least three days after moving. If he or she gets outside of their new home, they just cannot find their way back because they have not become re-oriented.

FLIGHT OF THE PUSSYWILLOW

CHAPTER FIVE

THE car had been washed and polished and was all ready and waiting for the three of us. The oil had been checked, the gas tank was full, and on this beautiful summer morning Sindhi and I were all ready, and we would call for Flora on the way downstairs. We bade the Family goodbye, with a hug for Fifi and Ku'ei, and reassurance from Buttercup that everything at home would be well looked after so there was no need for me to feel concern. A special message from the Guv who admonished us to be very careful and not to drive too fast. He patted Sindhi affectionately, telling her to be a good girl cat and that he would be missing her but that Ma would take good care of her he was sure. I had to admit (privately) that perhaps I had 'bitten off rather more than I could chew' in undertaking this trip (two hundred and sixty miles each way, and parts of the highway were not in too good a condition). However, it was too late to change my mind — the only thing to do was to go ahead and make the best of the situation.

Flora settled herself in the driver's seat and I sat with Sindhi in the back of the car. Since we were starting early we were not hampered by other traffic on the road. Therefore, we relaxed and enjoyed the scenery and unpolluted morning air, and it never crossed my mind that I would be making the trip again within two or three months, with not one but three Cat People, in a different car and another driver. We sped along for something like an hour and a half and then noticed a roadside restaurant. It was adjoining a service station and seemed like a convenient place to stop for breakfast. Sindhi stayed in the car which we parked in the shade because a closed car can become extremely uncomfortable for a little cat on a hot summer day. After we had finished our meal we felt refreshed and ready to start off again, and so we continued along Highway 401 for mile after mile, through St. Thomas (the city — not the Saint), and on toward Fort Erie. Fortunately neither Flora nor I wanted to keep up a non-stop conversation and soon we were oblivious to our surroundings and lost each with our own thoughts. However, drivers seem to keep part of their mind on the mechanical aspect and, immediately there is a need for full consciousness they are instantly alert; otherwise they seem to 'tick over' — appearing to propel the vehicle automatically, just like a cat who apparently is sitting dreaming his life away but a slight sound will bring him back to full attention and action.

Although we had lived in Canada for almost two years, still we had not become used to the long distances people traveled, especially by car, on the roads. Two hundred and sixty miles was nothing to a Canadian, but to people such as I and my Family it seemed a very long way.

I wondered what was in Flora's mind for she too had had many experiences, not all of them pleasant. She was also a New Canadian, having emigrated from Europe. Her life had been full of obstacles and she was doing her best to carve herself a new life. I Would always entertain a warm feeling toward her because she had been one of our earliest contacts in this country: She had been instrumental in making our arrival more pleasant than it would have been, by her kindness in providing all the necessities for our immediate use in the furnished house we had rented. I can still picture the beautiful rosy apples which greeted us as we walked into the living room; however, now we have become accustomed to the pleasures of Canada's apples, peaches, and various other delights which this country produces.

My reverie undisturbed, Sindhi close beside me, I remembered Coralie (another young person who I had met in those early days). Coralie was a native Canadian, the first Canadian born person I had met. She was employed in a bank in Riverside Township, and nothing was ever too much trouble for her (which was a great help when everything was a bit different in this New Country).

After I had been to the bank a few times I saw she wanted to say something special to me, and she shyly volunteered the information that her Mother was an avid reader of the Guv's books. 'Oh yes', she continued, 'Mother enjoys the books immensely and she would really love to have one of her volumes autographed by him. Thus a pleasant association resulted which continued until after we left the Windsor area.

Thus I reminisced on the events since our arrival in North America. . . . I had often marveled at the thought of a person we knew in a store in Riverside who traveled sixty miles in an evening just to visit and to play cards, and then make the return journey (another sixty miles) to be at her place of work early the next morning. Then there was the Pet Shop Owner who we met fairly often when we called for Cat Nip or Cat litter, or some other small items of interest. This man had seen the Guv's name mentioned in an international magazine of some note, and I found it most amusing when he commented, 'But you cannot get a mention in there even if you pay.' At such times as these, with no particular problem of the moment to occupy one's thoughts, there seemed no end to the recollections which come to the surface: I recalled another impression of that Pet Shop. Two beautiful Siamese cats were there awaiting a home; they were fairly adult and I felt attracted to them. They were well past the kitten stage and I went close to the cage where they were, just to be sociable and to greet them. Then I realized they must have thought I was going to take them (and judging by their voices they must have been asking me to do so) and it saddened me that I was unable to do anything about it.

Perhaps one can be too sensitive about things, but I have always felt a certain remorse for approaching them and possibly raising their hopes for a moment, then appearing to let them down. I have often wondered about them and I strongly believe that Siamese cats especially should not be allowed to stay in a pet shop — that orders should be passed on to the breeder. They are too sensitive for the only kind of treatment pet stores are able to provide, and many stores will not contemplate detaining them in such conditions.

At last — we saw by the signposts that we were approaching Fort Erie and we sighed with relief — all of us now beginning to feel weary and getting tired of driving. Just before reaching the Fort Erie Hotel we noticed a sign indicating the Business Section; but it branched off to the left and we wanted to go straight ahead. Finally we arrived at the motel where we had made previous reservations (just across from the Fort Erie Hotel and situated a fair distance from the main shopping area). Fort Erie has two areas — it is in two parts: The south end, which is near the Niagara river (being the original older district), and the north end (newer) more modern, and the main shopping street is Jarvis Street.

We were staying nearer the older part and we had chosen a motel, deciding it would be easier for parking and more accessible for Sindhi's needs; also, we hoped fewer staff would intrude if she was to be left in the room alone.

We could have done very well with a rest because the temperature had climbed quite a lot by 2 o'clock in the afternoon; but, uncomfortably warm as we were and some- what exhausted, there was no time to lose, so we made Sindhi comfortable and then we drove off. We had been told about some places to rent in the south end; however, they did not seem to suit our requirements so we decided to go along to see the house on the Parkway. First of all, we returned to the motel to find Sindhi awake and rested, so we took her with us. Once more we passed the south end of the town, then past the foot of Jarvis Street, continuing along the Parkway until we came to Cedar House (the name had appealed to me and I was not disappointed when I saw it); it was built of cedar and I could hardly wait to look around the place.

Sindhi stayed in the car with Flora while I went to investigate. I noticed a few people wandering around the grounds throughout my investigation. Mrs. C. was waiting for me in the house and she was very helpful. She showed me around the rooms which were all on one floor, including a nice sun room which unfortunately was packed full with furniture.

Then we went into the basement to see the water hely hours. As we sped along the Highway my thoughts were of Home and the Family — four of them eagerly awaiting our return (we expected). My make-up being such that my Home means a great deal to me, I do not enjoy being away from it or leaving the Family for very long. It is not that I consider myself to be indispensable for there is no one who cannot be done without; it is merely that my nature demands stability and reliability, which my Home represents. I have not preferred the constant moving which has been our lot, but since there is nothing one can do about it I have ceased to worry, and have adopted the maxim, 'If you cannot change it — accept it.' Being of an imaginative nature I speculated on the reactions of the Family regarding this property I had just seen. Would they feel the same as I did and decide to give Cedar House a trial?

Personally, I hankered after the freedom it would offer — a house situated all by itself with no other dwelling close by, I visualized myself amongst the trees where, like Ferdinand the Bull, I might just sit and smell the flowers. From this it may be deduced that I am not an energetic person, not physically at any rate; but I do have a great affinity with tree life, and the Guv has increased my devotion with many interesting stories of their origin and purpose. I know that to be close to them induces harmony and tranquility (if one believes), and I know that they are indeed thinking entities. As we drove along I had a vivid memory of an incident when Silver Tabby lived with us. He spent many hours resting on a big branch of The Old Apple Tree, just by the back entrance in our little garden where we had lived in a London suburb. I remembered the Guv was having a telepathic conversation with Silver Tabby, as we all sat quietly in the room, when, expressing a look of surprise, the Guv asked audibly, 'However did you know that?' Immediately came the response, 'Well, I will tell you — Mr. Tree told it to me.'

Since that time I have held the Tree People in even higher regard. The American Indians had a great respect for trees and in their writings one can read of The Great Tree Spirit, who they held in deep veneration. Yes indeed, I hoped with great fervor that everyone would agree this was a move well worth considering.

CHAPTER SIX

It would not be strictly correct to say that our return journey was EN-TIRELY uneventful for, before we reached Windsor, the car 'conked out' — on the Walkerville road, a few miles from home. So my first greeting to the Family was by telephone, with a request for someone to come and collect Sindhi and me. Flora had to stay with the automobile until a mechanic could get out there and see if he could get it going; otherwise it would have to be towed away. Judging by Flora's expression I guessed that all was not well as we sped along, and the engine seemed to lack its natural 'purr'; but she did not comment until we actually came to a halt, and then she did say something . . .which I will not repeat here!! Later she admitted that, in her eagerness to reach home as quickly as possible, she had overdriven and the car just would not (or could not) make it. The Guv was most tolerant when I reported our predicament and he said it would not be long until a car would be there for us. Later he explained how a machine, or an instrument of any kind, will give far better service if you give it the attention it needs, plus a certain amount of understanding. Many people have commented on the Guv's magic touch when dealing with a car, a camera, and even a typewriter, when another person could do nothing with it. The Guv and the instrument seem to blend together and become one unit, and I have seen him produce really good pictures from an ordinary box camera when another person would do no better with a far superior instrument. Even the tools he uses receive the same treatment; I have never known him to put them away after use without the same care he reserves for a sophisticated piece of machinery, and it is not an exaggeration to say you would have to go a long way before finding such a perfectionist in whatever task was being undertaken.

Fifi and Ku'ei looked contented as though they had been well cared for in my absence (as they had been) and we were all happy to be together again. I was very proud of Ku'ei who had never spent more than a very few nights of her life without me. Once when she was quite young the Guv and I had found it necessary to be away together for twenty-four hours, and on our return we were told she had taken no food at all. It certainly gave us a fright, so never again did we both go away at the same time unless it was for only a few hours. It was quite obvious that if our trip had lasted another twenty-four hours Miss Ku'ei would no longer have been at home to greet us.

The Guv had a private conversation with Sindhi and I didn't dare think of the interpretation she was placing on that outing — how she was describing her experiences. She probably said, 'Thank heaven I'm back with you Guv and not cavorting around the countryside with those crazy women. I did hear a whisper though, that she had found the trip to be so long she was sure she had been all the way to Vancouver!

After some discussion, and having made the big decision to uproot ourselves again — everybody agreeing it would be for the best, we began to look forward to the move with pleasurable anticipation. What a change it would be to get away from all the Riverside Drive distractions where, just below our windows, traffic went speeding by at all hours of the day and night. At the other side of the road were the railroad tracks — and it was almost at the end of the line, so with trains passing by and the shunting which went on, there was hardly a quiet moment. Ocean going ships, lakers and local craft on the Detroit river added to the pandemonium and when the Cat People went into hiding at the sound of the frequent foghorn blasts, we felt like doing the same.

Really there was much to commend this change, and everybody believed it would be a successful move so we began to make preparations. One important item was what to do about our furniture which we had bought the previous year, and while not wildly expensive or elaborate, was still something we owned. There would be very few things we could take with us to a furnished house which was not very big and already crowded, so what could we do? Our first idea was to approach the owner of the store where it had been purchased (which we did), and to our surprise and utter dismay we were informed in a not too polite manner that there was no demand for used furniture and he was just not interested. If this was true of Windsor, we found other parts of the country to be somewhat more reasonable in this respect; or perhaps we had just been unfortunate in our first experience. However, it's an ill wind that profits no one, and we were able to assist a young man who, having just got married, was having difficulty in getting a home together.

FLIGHT OF THE PUSSYWILLOW

He was very pleased to accept our offer, and so it was arranged that on our departure he would take all but the very few small personal items which we would need ourselves. We had reached the point where we almost expected to have to pay someone to take the goods away, so the young man had helped us too in removing them. He had done us one or two favors in the past, so it was a case of 'one good turn deserves another'.

How is it that a family can accumulate so many possessions in the course of a few months, I wondered. Certainly we were no exception, and I was reminded of it the other day on hearing that Mrs. Ford, the President's wife, had to go back to their old home in Virginia to do a lot of sorting out in the attic, or something, before finally settling into the White House. Well, no doubt the President's wife had a lot more sorting out to do than we had, and she had only one (instead of three) Siamese to help her but Top Cat 'Shan' was probably already well installed and performing important duties at 1600 Pennsylvania Avenue. Anyhow we certainly found a great deal of unnecessary paraphernalia, and after disposing of it we were lighter in spirit, as well as possessions, while vowing that never again would we give way to hoarding articles which we did not need.

Everything was planned for our departure in the early part of September, the first week if possible as we were eager to get to what would be our new home — the place where we would be staying for at least six months with an option to continue the tenancy on a monthly basis. The Guv's book was completed and in the hands of the publisher so we were, in a way, 'ticking over' as far as our business and professional activities were concerned.

Our traveling arrangements were all in order, particularly regarding preparations for the Cat People. A friend, Mrs. Ruth Durr (or just 'Ruth' as she had come to be known to us), had offered to drive me (along with Fifi, Ku'ei and Sindhi) in her fairly big, if not so new, blue car. So that was a great help and we were delighted to accept her offer because we had been wondering how we would manage. The Cat People liked Ruth and they treated her as one of the Family because she spent a good part of the day in part of our house, which she used as an office while she was waiting for her own store to be completed. Her supplies had be into the sun room was wide open and Sindhi Cat had obviously been amusing herself at my expense. Although we sat down to a very simple meal consisting of a few supplies we had brought along, we really enjoyed it, followed by a nice pot of tea to which Ruth was very partial, and soon she decided to retire as she had to get back to Windsor the next day and attend to some business matters regarding the store.

By this time the Cat People were beginning to look rather weary, and the Little One was quite restless and somewhat irritable, so I debated the problem of how best to get us all settled for the night. In the end I decided to put Sindhi in the Master bedroom and stay with her for a time until she felt a little more rested, and then I would share the chesterfield in the living room with Fifi and Ku'ei. I noticed a big armchair also which the Cat People might find a bit more comfortable if Ma should prove to be restless. Before going to sleep I thought I would have a little session with my small radio, and I knew the programs would be coming from Niagara Falls or Welland while the main newscasts would be relayed from Toronto. Fort Erie did not have a radio station but that was not important for it was quite simple to tune in to Buffalo, New York, which was just across the river, and we later enjoyed some very good programs from that city.

But on that first night, all my efforts were doomed to failure. No matter what I did I couldn't get a sound out of the thing — it seemed quite dead. I shook it, twiddled the knobs, and finally gave up in frustration and weariness, deciding to try the Land of Dreams instead, with the intention of putting my radio problem before the Guv who would have no difficulty in solving it. But dreams do not come to order and in the darkness I found myself drifting around and remembering past experiences; some pleasant, others not so pleasant, and some probably not even worthy of recording.

At one period of my life I had used a certain method of inducing sleep which usually worked; it was a process of 'regressing' my thoughts, thinking back — back — and further back on the events of my life, and usually I didn't get very far before achieving the desired effect — SLEEP. Later I reasoned that it was not advisable to indulge in this practice so I gave it up in favor of looking to the future; looking forward and making plans with the intention of improving the days ahead instead of just reliving the past which, I decided, gets one nowhere. Besides, now I am able to induce the state of sleep by complete relaxation which I have learned through the Guv's books. So why work hard at something when you can achieve better results with less effort? Now I compromise with myself when resting for a few minutes, or even in going about my routine duties. I allow myself to day-dream a little and take a peep into the past, otherwise how can I hope to improve the future (and as that system was presumably used by the old Atlanteans, how could I hope to improve on it), and this way I find the practice a pleasant and useful form of relaxation.

So, while not in a deep sleep but just hovering near the border, I felt myself drifting around, wondering about the future and how it would compare with the past. Life in Ireland (that remnant of Atlantis) had been very enjoyable, living as we did by the sea, on the Hill facing Ireland's Eye and Lambay Island, and the Mountains of Mourne away in the distance but not always visible. We had taken a drive one evening around the Hill of Howth and that was how we spied this 'House for Rent' sign, and the welcoming cry of the sea gulls made us feel at home. The memories of Howth came flooding into my consciousness and I remembered how the Guv used to let himself down the side of the cliff on the end of a rope. He used to enjoy 'exploring' the caves which were there at sea level, and I used to think it must bring back many happy thoughts of his younger years.

The Guv was more agile at that time and he was able to take walks around the garden with Fifi and Ku'ei who loved to accompany him; and I used to take pictures of the Family. But cats do not enjoy being photographed — not our cats anyhow.

We were living in this particular house when we found Fifi, or did Fifi find us? And for that reason alone I would reserve a special place in my heart for Ben Edair, the little house which for a time provided a measure of peace and sanctuary for us.

From a place somewhat higher a little plateau on the Hill, I had taken a short cine film of the Guv where, first he sat on a rock where I took a 'close-up', and then he walked toward me, and the result was very pleasing even though the equipment we had used was quite modest. The beautiful blue of the sky, blending with the saffron of the robes created a delightful effect and we derived much pleasure from viewing it on the big screen, on which we showed slides and short cine films in the evenings. The Irish people had been very friendly towards us and I always felt an affinity with them; and the Guv and I used to enjoy listening to many of the Irish songs — one Irish lullaby having a great appeal for us.

Personally I had always found great pleasure and satisfaction in listening to the recordings of John McCormick, the Irish tenor. His voice seemed to soothe my nerves and raise my 'vibrations' (a much overworked word these days) . . so with all these pleasant memories flooding my mind on that first night it was not surprising that I woke up feeling refreshed and contented, though my sleep had been 'fitful'.

Later that morning I remembered another episode which had not been so pleasant: It was one evening when the Guv said he would take me out in one of the dinghies, which could be rented down by Howth Harbor and which was powered by an outboard motor. For a time we were really enjoying the trip when gradually an eerie feeling pervaded the atmosphere. Dusk seemed to be descending prematurely, and then suddenly a squall blew up and we had to turn towards the shore as fast as we could. It was not until we reached home that I realized how serious and in what great danger we had been, and how it had taken all the Guv's energy and know-how to prevent us from capsizing and being carried away — probably disappearing forever. What a responsibility it would have been for Buttercup (who ex- pressed great relief on our return) had she been left with two poor orphaned Siamese People; and how distressing for Fifi and Ku'ei.

We breakfasted a little late and Ruth said she had spent a comfortable night, having been supervised periodically when a cat would walk over her bed to check and see whether she was still breathing. After breakfast she suggested driving along to the grocery store in the town to get a few provisions which we urgently needed, and while she was away I tidied up around the house as much as I could.

On her return (which was around eleven o'clock) she had a light lunch because she wanted to leave no later than midday; but she was hoping to see the Guv before leaving and we had no idea of the exact time he would arrive. So I went out with Ruth to her car and at that moment, almost as though planned, just coming up to the entrance was the easily idble pink and gold Mercury bearing the Guv, with Buttercup at the wheel — just in time to say 'Hello' and 'Goodbye'.

At last the Family were together again, so we all sat down and reported our experiences since leaving Windsor. Nothing too exciting seemed to have happened to any of us fortunately, though we did remember one or two small details which had not been attended to before our departure.

But it was a simple matter to telephone the owners who lost no time in dealing with these simple problems. My radio was standing on the table and the Guv asked me how I had found the programs and whether I had listened to anything special, or if I had found any one station better than

FLIGHT OF THE PUSSYWILLOW

another. Rather sheepishly I had to admit that I could not pass an opinion since the 'so-and-so' radio had refused to work for me. And I really did feel like a sheep when he examined the thing and found the batteries had been put in the wrong way 'round. Ah well, I thought, we live and learn.

After that problem had been dealt with we were eager to take a good look around the place, so when the Guv was ready we went exploring — first of all down to the basement to look at the hot water and heating arrangements. The Guv examined everything carefully while the 'People' poked their noses into every nook and cranny. We were interested to see a workbench, fitted with tools, which showed that Mrs. C's late husband must have been something of a carpenter; but we were not at all interested in a billiard table which, in our opinion, occupied too much space. So we moved it to one side of the room, much to the chagrin of Mrs. C. when she found out (it seems that a billiard table has to be set up very accurately and we had really revealed our ignorance in treating it in such a thoughtless manner, when she had paid someone to install it).

The Cat People often went down to the basement, ostensibly to catch a mouse, and sometimes we wondered who would run the fastest, mouse or cat, if by chance they did encounter such a creature. Since they looked upon themselves as People and not Cats, one hoped they would not allow a mouse to chase THEM.

Each of the Cats wore a haver as often as possible, and we were fortunate that year in that the warm weather lasted until about November. Mrs. C. had taken away the screens from the windows and put up the extra 'double' windows in preparation for the winter, but the temperature remained so high that we had to revert to the summer arrangement and put back the screens until almost the end of the year.

Sindhi took several boating excursions with us, and she behaved very well but her temperament continued to be unreliable, so we still felt greatly concerned about her. The warm autumn days were conducive to idling on the water; and on occasion we would just drift in the other direction, up the creek instead of down into the main river.

Sindhi seemed to enjoy these outings, at least she did not protest, though she probably kept private her real thoughts on the matter. If the Guv was not going out, and there was shopping to do, I would accompany Buttercup, and Sindhi would go along too, sometimes going as far as Niagara Falls which was bigger than Fort Erie and therefore enjoyed a greater variety of stores. There were no stores close by Cedar House so it was necessary to take the car each time shopping had to be done. It was interesting to note the different foods each girl cat liked best. Fifi always enjoyed lobster (canned lobster) which seemed to contain everything necessary for her physical well-being, and since she had been half-starved during the greater part of her existence, it was necessary to see that she had all she nerness and lead when she went outside so we were able to maintain a proper check on their movements. The harness was exactly that and not just a collar around the neck, with a lead attached, but with pieces of leather fitting around the 'arms', providing a comfortable effect even if it became necessary to give a slight 'tug' occasionally. Until a cat gets used to being 'harnessed' it is not unusual for the creature to sit down, refusing to move; and in Miss Ku'ei's case it took a good deal of time and patience before she acceded to the arrangement. Of course the procedure was introduced in kittenhood and later she would never dream of going outside without being 'dressed'.

It was not long before Mrs. Fifi Greywhiskers was shinning up a tree, and the Guv was almost having a heart attack in case she would break away and climb so high that we would not be able to reach her. Of course, we attached a piece of twine to the end of the lead, which was not long enough to satisfy her, and there were times when we had to run into the garage and fetch a ladder to assist us in rescuing her. It had long been Fifi's ambition to do some tree-climbing and she was going to make the most of the opportunity while it lasted. When she began to get tired she would rest on a wide branch (of course the Guv always chose the most suitable trees for her exercises), and knowing how little pleasure she had ever had, it gave us pleasure too to see her sitting there with an expression of absolute content — and a definite air of achievement.

Miss Ku'ei and Miss Sindhi were not so interested in tree- climbing but they loved investigating on the ground and playing with the various hued autumn leaves which were beginning to fall fairly rapidly now. Looking back on those weeks before the advent of winter, one is left with a delightful sense of satisfaction in the knowledge that those little people had had such a happy time out-of-doors, which was something they had all missed in their earlier life.

FLIGHT OF THE PUSSYWILLOW

CHAPTER EIGHT

The Guv was eager to try out the dinghy which was moored in the little creek, just down a few steps and close to the rear entrance of the house. So, at the first opportunity I was pleased to accompany him. We decided to make the trial trip without other passengers, just to be sure everything was safe and in good working order (and we had not forgotten our experience in Ireland when we were caught in a squall). Out of the creek we moved into the Niagara river; and everything went well so we spent an enjoyable time. I was not too afraid to go on the water because in an emergency I would be able to swim a little, and I knew the Guv would see that nothing too awful would happen to us. Of course, I may have had a few subconscious reservations because once I had almost drowned, and would have done so had there not been someone at hand to rescue me immediately. And another experience which had caused amusement in spite of my predicament, was on a river in England when, for some reason, I and my boating companion were going to moor our boat. While I was reaching out to pull the boat in it gradually drifted away and I found myself in the water, feeling very undignified and altogether miserable, while my companion could do little to help, being overcome with a fit of laughter at the sight of me slowly slipping out of the boat and drenched to the waist. The situation must have been cause for mirth to the onlooker, but it left me chilled and not very amiable until at last I had to laugh also.

Well, we took trips on the Niagara river as often as possible, and we were fortunate that year in that the warm weather lasted until about November. Mrs. C. had taken away the screens from the windows and put up the extra 'double' windows in preparation for the winter, but the temperature remained so high that we had to revert to the summer arrangement and put back the screens until almost the end of the year.

FLIGHT OF THE PUSSYWILLOW

Sindhi took several boating excursions with us, and she behaved very well but her temperament continued to be unreliable, so we still felt greatly concerned about her. The warm autumn days were conducive to idling on the water; and on occasion we would just drift in the other direction, up the creek instead of down into the main river.

Sindhi seemed to enjoy these outings, at least she did not protest, though she probably kept private her real thoughts on the matter. If the Guv was not going out, and there was shopping to do, I would accompany Buttercup, and Sindhi would go along too, sometimes going as far as Niagara Falls which was bigger than Fort Erie and therefore enjoyed a greater variety of stores. There were no stores close by Cedar House so it was necessary to take the car each time shopping had to be done. It was interesting to note the different foods each girl cat liked best. Fifi always enjoyed lobster (canned lobster) which seemed to contain everything necessary for her physical well-being, and since she had been half-starved during the greater part of her existence, it was necessary to see that she had all she needed to keep her going in her later days. Canned lobster is far too costly these days, but when Fifi was with us we always managed to keep her supplies adequate and, apart from the solid part, she also loved the liquid which to her was 'Lobster Wine'. Ku'ei was not greatly interested in food, and she was a most adaptable person in this respect. Having moved from one country to another it had been necessary to take whatever each country had to offer; thus, at one period she enjoyed rabbit cooked in a pressure cooker, which she considered very succulent, but when rabbit was not obtainable she would switch to chicken or fish, and she would take her food in a most polite manner.

Ku'ei was a most dainty person and her table manners matched her appearance, but on occasion I would marvel at the sight of this apparently fragile creature manipulating a big chunk of chicken, perhaps a leg, grasped tightly between her teeth, head held high so that the meat did not touch the floor, marching off to a quiet corner where she might really get down to a good meal without interference and audience. To digress a little from the problem of food I must put on record that Miss Ku'ei had the most beautiful features which any cat (or human for that matter) might envy, and each time I had to prise open her mouth to give her vitamins or other medication, or even spoon feed her when she was sick, I never ceased to marvel at her beautifully shaped mouth, and I gloried in the delicate beauty of MY CAT. Her coloring was a little darker than the normal seal point, probably due to

FLIGHT OF THE PUSSYWILLOW

the fact that her father was a 'chocolate soldier' (a chocolate point Siamese), while her mother was a seal point. Her eyes, like those of Elizabeth Taylor, were a deep violet — a color which has been declared 'very unusual'.

In my enthusiasm for Ku'ei and her beauty, my affection for Fifi and Sindhi was no less and never wavered. Fifi was probably the sweetest natured Cat Person we had ever known, her thoughts were constantly fixed on the welfare of others and she never desired anything for herself. As for Baby Sindhi, wasn't she my Big Responsibility, and so charming in her own spey something large like a pigeon or a gull. She would become quite excited and, with a muttering sort of 'chatter', was probably telling the bird to 'Just wait until I can get a hold of you — you will provide a beautiful meal for me!' One always hoped these remarks were not meant to be taken seriously.

FLIGHT OF THE PUSSYWILLOW

CHAPTER NINE

As the days gradually shortened and the evenings seemed longer we all retired earlier, each to our own room so there was more opportunity for reading and listening to the radio. Miss Sindhi, like my shadow, was never very far away from me — my thought was that if she stayed right beside me with the door closed I could devote the greater part of my attention to reading or listening to a radio program. Towards the end of the day one needs to put aside the strains and stresses of the day and be able to enjoy a little period of relaxation without interruption. Unfortunately this does not seem possible for many people, or possibly they do not realize the necessity of a quiet period occasionally — how it would assist them in coping with their problems and making their lives altogether more enjoyable, and fulfilling.

So, knowing there would be no feline hissing or spitting, Sindhi and I were able to make the most of each other's company since no one else was likely to intrude. Miss Ku'ei put up with this state of affairs for some time (not very happily I felt), and then she gradually asserted her authority in a quiet sort of way. At first she would come into the room, along with Sindhi and me, and she would settle herself down on a chair on one side of my bed, or on my bed (with Sindhi on the other side) and stay for short periods only.

When Sindhi became too restless Ku'ei just had to leave and join Fifi on the chesterfield in the Guv's room, where she would spend the remainder of the night. But Miss Ku'ei was quite a determined young lady, as are most persons born in July, and in the end she had so completely regained her position that she was once again staying all night with Sindhi and me; thus the Guv had become Mrs. Fifi's sole responsibility during the hours of darkness, a situation which gave her the greatest possible satisfaction. I sometimes wondered whatever must have been said to the poor little Sindhi Cat to make her tolerate Ku'ei's intrusion into Sindhi's quiet time with Ma. Perhaps it was just as well I did not know what had been said for no doubt it would have made my ears burn, so I would never know whether it was from a sense of apprehension as to what her fate might be if she continued in her truculent attitude, or whether she just decided that 'the battle was not worth the effort'. But the end result seemed satisfactory for these two settled down into a sort of armed neutrality.

If cats are subject to the same influences as human animals, then Ku'ei must have spent many miserable moments through being 'shut away' from her Ma. Being a Siamese she had a double reason for being unhappy about the position, for Siamese People are noted for their trait of possessiveness; they usually expect to be a 'One Person Cat' as far as humans are concerned, and they do not easily tolerate competition from others of their own species. Often a Siamese will be just as happy in the company of a dog, but there is one exception regarding the possessive attitude. If one has two kittens of the same age, and even of the same litter, they will each accept the other without malice, and indeed they will often spend a happier life than one Cat Person all alone, especially if human attention is not readily available — or if the cat would be left on his own for long periods. Like Siamese, July born people often suffer very greatly through a feeling of loneliness — a fear of being misunderstood, or even not being understood at all. In some ways these people may be looked upon as the martyrs of the world, and sometimes they will consider themselves as such. they will work around the problem (or project) until they have attained the desired goal, be it a situation or an object upon which their mind is set. In this respect Miss Ku'ei was very 'human-like', and also in the way she would display great affection for the person whose cat she understood herself to be, more than to another person — just as many July born 'Human Animals' are (so to speak) 'one-person cats'.

The so-called master bedroom was stuffy and I never really got to feel 'at home' or 'comfortable' in those surroundings, though it could have been worse except for the fact that I tend to live more in my mind than in my surroundings. If my mind is fairly free of problems I am not greatly concerned with my surroundings because, usually, my thoughts are in another dimension. Still, the room was a bit depressing, set low on the ground; consequently always rather dark, with a feeling of dampness, and anything but a friendly atmosphere. When the lights were out and the curtains drawn aside (after we had gone to bed) I used to amuse myself by watching the traffic passing

FLIGHT OF THE PUSSYWILLOW

along the Parkway, by the edge of the river. Of course I had to keep the curtains drawn on the occasions when I was going to do some reading because the house, although set in its own grounds, was not sufficiently secluded to preclude curious onlookers and those who are known by the horrible title of 'Peeping Tom'.

Even though it means doing a bit of trespassing, certain people do not seem to be able to resist the urge to pry into the private lives of others, especially if the 'attraction' is a lighted room with drapes undrawn. Cedar House was no exception.

It was nice to listen to the radio and we did this fairly often while watching the traffic; and the Cat People seemed to enjoy the musical program, but the broadcasts which stayed most clearly in my mind were the talks preceding the United States presidential election. Listening to the Republican candidate, Nixon, it would seem that only by voting Republican and continuing on the lines of the Eisenhower administration could America survive. Then there would be the young Democrat, Kennedy, apparently full of charm and persuasiveness, advocating a complete change. So it was no wonder the voters were a bit confused, perplexed, and left wondering who would really serve the country best. It has always interested me to hear of the promises each candidate makes in the hope of being elected. So these talks were no exception, especially in the light of subsequent events.

Each of those candidates has had an opportunity to exercise his skill as President of the United States, and most people would have found it hard to believe that, within the span of less than a decade and a half, both of them would be out of office due to forces beyond their control. Richard Nixon must often have regretted continuing in the political arena, following the time he lost the Governorship of California when he declared, 'Well, you won't have Richard Nixon to push around any more.' Those words were directed to the press of course and one is left wondering, just a few weeks after his resignation as President, whether he will ever again enjoy a measure of peace; or will he have to endure being 'pushed around' for the remainder of his days. Whave committed, surely there must be a limit to the shame, embarrassment and persecution they are expected to endure. And those who are so prone to judge and pronounce sentence are not always so free of guilt as they would appear.

The campaign period of the early sixties came to mind again this week when it was announced that the last of the Kennedy brothers had found it necessary to abandon all thoughts of entering the presidential, or vice-presidential, race in 1976 — he had decided he could not contemplate running for either position two years from now. Considering the fate of his two elder brothers this was obviously the most sensible, and indeed the only decision left, for after all who amongst us is anxious to go headlong into disaster when the warning is crystal clear?

By this time the mornings were becoming quite cool, and we felt rather sad when we thought of the rapidly approaching winter months. But it was still warm enough to take the Cat People outside in what was now a 'fall' sunshine. Buttercup and I had quite a time keeping these creatures in check since they had more energy now that it was cooler. They were as lively as three young horses, and they would have enjoyed more than anything to break away from their leashes and, like young horses, gallop away into the distance. On some of the colder days Sindhi and Ku'ei would go out driving with the Guv and me; Sindhi having been told she would have to behave herself — or else!!! Mrs. Fifi would stay home with Buttercup.

If we wanted to take longer than just a few minutes drive we might go as far as Welland, which was about the same distance as Niagara Falls, where we would pass along by the Welland Canal (which is part of the Great Lakes Waterway). Another place we might visit was beyond Fort Erie, right along Garrison Road, a few miles further than the Fort Erie Hotel. This was a little community by the name of Crystal Beach — a well-known holiday resort populated in the summer months by many United States residents who owned summer cottages there by the river and, during the tourist season, very noisy with its various 'fair' type attractions.

It was during this period that we decided it might be a good idea to have a different car; perhaps something a little more economical since the Mercury had needed a fair amount of 'attention'; and its gasoline consumption was considerable. It was a bigger vehicle than we really needed, so we cast around for something smaller. After the usual Family discussion we contacted a company in Niagara Falls and arranged for the proprietor to come to our house so that we might have his opinion on the matter. Finally, after some negotiation, we found ourselves the owners of a little Renault — a car of French manufacture which was approved of by Mrs. Fifi (being of French extraction herself) who considered it would provide good service, though she was not planning to travel in it unless absolutely necessary.

FLIGHT OF THE PUSSYWILLOW

The acquisition of this little car brought back memories of one or two episodes in Ireland which had caused us a good deal of amusement and which, even as I recall them so long afterwards, I am unable to suppress a chuckle. I feel sure that the Guv, with his acute sense of humor, will not object to these incidents being included in the 'Sindhi' story. While living in Howth, near Dublin (well, not more than a dozen miles from that city), we had a visitor — a bearded young man, and one day he turned up at our house with a new car, a small affair which he called a 'Bubble' — or something.

Anyway it seemed to us a most odd contraption, and one had to pull open the plastic roof before one was able to get inside the 'machine'. (Before going any further I have to say that, 'Yes, I do have the Guv's permission to tell the story.' Well . . ., I just informed him that he had given me the go-ahead!!!) This vehicle was only a two-seater, at most, and the Guv received an invitation to accompany the bearded young man and 'take a spin' around the countryside. The Guv, never averse to a fresh experience, agreed of course — even if he did look askance at this strange device. As they left, Buttercup and I had to smile at the sight of them — apparently enclosed in a plastic dome. It was not until they returned, however, that we were made aware of the really amusing part: The weather being warm, they had opened the roof (and since the inside space was so limited they no doubt needed the extra air) and they went driving right away beyond the city, enjoying the scenery and probably absorbed in an interesting conversation. Suddenly the Guv realized they had violated a traffic regulation by making a crossing at a red light (and of course there just HAD to be a guardia, an Irish policeman, around). The two occupants sat there in anticipation, waiting for the guardia to come over to them and issue a ticket. And eventually he arrived — but it seemed that the sight of those two bearded 'characters' seated in that small 'Bubble' was just too much for the officer who was so overcome with mirth that he could only cover his face with one hand while he waved them on, and he himself turned away before they could see his almost uncontrolled laughter! Perhaps this is not such a dignified term to apply to the Guv, but perhaps he will forgive me since my intentions are respectful, but I have to admit (and it cannot be denied) that he is a 'good sport' for he daringly accepted a second esidential, or vice-presidential, race in 1976 — he had decided he could not contemplate running for either position two years from now. Considering the fate of his two elder brothers this was obviously the most sensible, and indeed the only decision left, for after all who amongst

41

us is anxious to go headlong into disaster when the warning is crystal clear?

By this time the mornings were becoming quite cool, and we felt rather sad when we thought of the rapidly approaching winter months. But it was still warm enough to take the Cat People outside in what was now a 'fall' sunshine. Buttercup and I had quite a time keeping these creatures in check since they had more energy now that it was cooler. They were as lively as three young horses, and they would have enjoyed more than anything to break away from their leashes and, like young horses, gallop away into the distance. On some of the colder days Sindhi and Ku'ei would go out driving with the Guv and me; Sindhi having been told she would have to behave herself — or else!!! Mrs. Fifi would stay home with Buttercup.

If we wanted to take longer than just a few minutes drive we might go as far as Welland, which was about the same distance as Niagara Falls, where we would pass along by the Welland Canal (which is part of the Great Lakes Waterway). Another place we might visit was beyond Fort Erie, right along Garrison Road, a few miles further than the Fort Erie Hotel. This was a little community by the name of Crystal Beach — a well-known holiday resort populated in the summer months by many United States residents who owned summer cottages there by the river and, during the tourist season, very noisy with its various 'fair' type attractions.

It was during this period that we decided it might be a good idea to have a different car; perhaps something a little more economical since the Mercury had needed a fair amount of 'attention'; and its gasoline consumption was considerable. It was a bigger vehicle than we really needed, so we cast around for something smaller. After the usual Family discussion we contacted a company in Niagara Falls and arranged for the proprietor to come to our house so that we might have his opinion on the matter. Finally, after some negotiation, we found ourselves the owners of a little Renault — a car of French manufacture which was approved of by Mrs. Fifi (being of French extraction herself) who considered it would provide good service, though she was not planning to travel in it unless absolutely necessary.

The acquisition of this little car brought back memories of one or two episodes in Ireland which had caused us a good deal of amusement and which, even as I recall them so long afterwards, I am unable to suppress a chuckle. I feel sure that the Guv, with his acute sense of humor, will not object to these incidents being included in the 'Sindhi' story. While living in

FLIGHT OF THE PUSSYWILLOW

Howth, near Dublin (well, not more than a dozen miles from that city), we had a visitor — a bearded young man, and one day he turned up at our house with a new car, a small affair which he called a 'Bubble' — or something.

Anyway it seemed to us a most odd contraption, and one had to pull open the plastic roof before one was able to get inside the 'machine'. (Before going any further I have to say that, 'Yes, I do have the Guv's permission to tell the story.' Well . . ., I just informed him that he had given me the go-ahead!!!) This vehicle was only a two-seater, at most, and the Guv received an invitation to accompany the bearded young man and 'take a spin' around the countryside. The Guv, never averse to a fresh experience, agreed of course — even if he did look askance at this strange device. As they left, Buttercup and I had to smile at the sight of them — apparently enclosed in a plastic dome. It was not until they returned, however, that we were made aware of the really amusing part: The weather being warm, they had opened the roof (and since the inside space was so limited they no doubt needed the extra air) and they went driving right away beyond the city, enjoying the scenery and probably absorbed in an interesting conversation. Suddenly the Guv realized they had violated a traffic regulation by making a crossing at a red light (and of course there just HAD to be a guardia, an Irish policeman, around). The two occupants sat there in anticipation, waiting for the guardia to come over to them and issue a ticket. And eventually he arrived — but it seemed that the sight of those two bearded 'characters' seated in that small 'Bubble' was just too much for the officer who was so overcome with mirth that he could only cover his face with one hand while he waved them on, and he himself turned away before they could see his almost uncontrolled laughter! Perhaps this is not such a dignified term to apply to the Guv, but perhaps he will forgive me since my intentions are respectful, but I have to admit (and it cannot be denied) that he is a 'good sport' for he daringly accepted a second invitation, and the second incident occurred right in the middle of the bridge which spans the river Liffey — right in the city of Dublin itself. This time, on the O'Connell Bridge, in the center of the city, apparently the clutch had burned out, for the car suddenly stalled and was full of dense white smoke. The driver (our bearded young man) apparently panicked, stepped out, slammed the door and walked away, leaving the Guv to deal with the guardia who, quite naturally, appeared on the scene. Happily, the Irish police officers are very tolerant, and not without a sense of humor either.

43

FLIGHT OF THE PUSSYWILLOW

Reverting to the subject of beards, we had a few un- pleasant experiences in the early days due to ignorance on the part of some of the young people of North America. Especially do I remember an occasion at Crystal Beach when we were standing by the car, where we had parked near a drug store, and I was just going inside the store when a group of youths began to make movements as though they were stroking an imaginary beard, and their remarks (anything but polite) were meant to be heard by us. Yes, the Guv wore a beard for a special reason — he had suffered a dam- aged jaw. But now it seems that we have come 'full circle' and beards no longer are a subject of ribald remarks but are being sported by just those types who scoffed at us.

FLIGHT OF THE PUSSYWILLOW

CHAPTER TEN

THERE is one big advantage in owning a mini-automobile and that is the ease with which one may find a parking space; but there is also a big danger too in that someone in a much larger car may be speeding along without noticing the 'mini', and it would be a dreadful thing to find oneself disappearing underneath such a vehicle. However, thanks to a kind fate we suffered no such experience while that little car was in our possession, and we enjoyed its compact cosiness; but it must have caused something of a problem for the Guv who was somewhat 'bulky', and it must have been rather a problem positioning himself in its small space. At any rate, this little 'box' served our purpose for some months, and it was disposed of only because we were going to be out of the country for a time and we could not take it with us.

As I contemplate these pages I relive once more those days at Cedar House. It is now October and the same time of the year as when we used to 'tootle' around the roads and the ground of the Niagara strip; often we seemed to be moving very fast and making a lot of noise, but we never reached our destination very quickly. The little car was rather like a little person — all fuss and bustle. But we liked our little Renault, even if Miss Ku'ei would have chosen a Volkswagen instead, preferably a red one.

It was beginning to get colder too, just as it is now here in Calgary, and as one gets older in years it is not a time to look forward to, for one's blood is thinner and it is harder to keep warm. As I look out of the window of the apartment building (which is our home) I see signs of early October frost and snow and, having been out collecting the mail already, I have also FELT the effects of the sudden change in temperature. But no doubt the body's metabolism will quickly adjust to this change. Just across the street, to the left, we are witnessing another sign of CHANGE, and the Guv too feels sad to see a group of little houses undergoing the process of demolition. The 'wreckers' can bring down one of these small dwellings within the space of thirty minutes and I can see the Guv's feelings reflected in his expression:

FLIGHT OF THE PUSSYWILLOW

'Houses, like people and animals, are created; live out their life-span and, again like people, having suffered through the strains and stresses of "living" become outdated and, thus, have to pass away to make room for something more modern and more suitable for the times.' Each morning I pass a few of these dwellings and I gaze upon them with longing, though I could not imagine myself living in one of them having become accustomed to apartment style life, but I still feel the past joy of ones own home with its little garden where one might plant one's feet firmly upon the earth, and enjoy the comfort of a grassy lawn. Hardly a day goes by without bringing to mind the words of my fellow countryman as I pass these little places: I can hear the echo of Thomas Hood who 'remembered the house where he was born', and how there was 'the little window where the sun came peeping in at morn'. Poetry and daydreaming may be out-of-place these days but my case seems to be incurable, and I do not think I would want it to be different. As the Guv intimates: 'So long as we are aware of the dividing line between daydreaming and reality we have little to worry about — we are not in serious trouble for, after all, we have to THINK before we can act, and if we can make our dreams come true then perhaps we have achieved something.' I like to think that is how it goes!

Today our friends, the sparrows, look a little dejected — they have not become accustomed to the cold weather either, and they are sad to see their shelters being torn down, for trees are very sparse here so the eaves of houses provide a measure of protection for bird-life.

As I walked around the block this morning attending to my errands, with the snowflakes dancing over my face, one small 'doggie' seemed to be enjoying a morning walk with his Master. Today in particular I was thinking of 'nature creatures' so I took a packet of bread crumbs to scatter on the waste spaces where cars are parked, or where demolition is finished and building has not yet begun. Why my special thoughts of nature today? Well I felt sorry for the little creatures crouched on the telephone wires, probably wondering how they were going to survive the cold of winter and whether anyone would pass on a few crumbs when the frosts came. I had another reason for wishing them happiness today for I remembered that this was the anniversary of the birth of Francis of Assisi (the patron saint of animals and all creatures of nature).

Most of us have an ideal, one person who they admire more than any other, and in my own case if there was one entity I would wish to emulate, to formulate my life upon, it would be Francis of Assisi who gave up a life of comfort to devote himself to the good of his fellow men, and who was especially dedicated to the creatures of nature who he loved and was loved by them in return. Birds used to perch on his shoulder, and he would address them as 'little brothers'. On occasion he would wait for them to finish their 'chatter' before continuing a discourse with the human creatures who gathered around him. There is in existence a beautiful Prayer attributed to St. Francis and hardly a year-end passes without someone sending me a copy, which I always feel would be worth applying to one's own life. Since I learned that this Prayer originated in Tibet it has an even greater significance for me than ever, and I realize how much we owe to those who have brought from that once mysterious land so many pearls of wisdom and ideas for good living; not least of these is our Guv, Lobsang Rampa. I have in my possession a wooden figure of my 'ideal', brought from Italy naturally, and wearing the simple brown girdled robe of his Order, which is still worn by the Franciscan fraternity. This figure has a bird perched on the shoulder and another creature resting at the feet, and I derive much inspiration and pleasure in its beauty and significance. I have heard this Assisan saint referred to as 'Probably the first of the flower people!!!' But was not the founder of the Christian religion one who flaunted convention and who, if He had lived in our present era, might well have been looked upon as a hippie? At least He had long hair, which is now frowned upon by the establishment; and he was definitely a pacifist, so . . . who are we to judge anyone after all.

A Prayer of St. Francis

Originally from Tibet

Lord, make me an instrument of Thy peace.

Where there is hate, may I bring love;

Where offense, may I bring pardon;

May I bring union in place of discord;

Truth, replacing error;

Faith, where once there was doubt;

Hope, for despair;

Light, where was darkness;

FLIGHT OF THE PUSSYWILLOW

Joy to replace sadness.

Make me not to so crave to be loved as to love.

Help me to learn that in giving I may receive;

In forgetting self, I may find life eternal.

Francis of Assisi

We are taught not to be envious of others but most of us suffer from this defect at one time or another (a human trait which we understand we must learn to overcome), and there are two special qualities about St. Francis that I admire, one of them being his beautiful singing voice. Before his so-called 'conversion' he was somewhat gay and carefree, and he would roam the streets with his friends, singing songs in a joyous mood, and his well-to-do-merchant father must have been very proud of his handsome and talented son. The second quality which I admire is the ability to 'tune in' to nature, to the elements, and become one with 'Brother Wind', 'Sister Moon', and the like. It was the same with all living creatures — they came to him without fear and with complete trust; and to Francis they were all his 'little sisters and brothers'. I confess to being envious of his ability to commune with them all, and if I am possessed of any ambition at all it is that one day I shall be able to commune with nature creatures by telepathy. I know that my cats, for instance, are fully aware of my thoughts, but it would be a wonderful thing to know EXACTLY what they are saying to ME instead of having to more or less hazard a guess as to their thoughts and needs. Yes, that is my goal.

In the compiling of these pages I seem to have fallen into the habit of digression, so I hope I am forgiven. At least I feel that I am in good company for the Guv freely admits to using this practice. I sincerely hope that I am not unconsciously copying his style for, not having his knowledge or his training, the result would be disastrous, and a very poor imitation indeed. If I should appear to have adopted any of his phrases I would like to state that it was not intentional; BUT, I would add that, having read and studied the fifteen volumes of the Guv's, it would be rather surprising if I had not 'absorbed' some of the author's expressions. If this shows too much I beg to be excused (and not accused) for any misdemeanor I may have committed.

My digressing seems to be digressing too far, so let us return to that October at Cedar House, which resembles this October in Calgary. The summer seemed to be extended indefinitely, as it is here this year. Two weeks ago we had snow and frost, while now we are experiencing an Indian Summer, which one hopes will also continue indefinitely.

We are about to revert to normal Mountain Time following the summer's Daylight Saving Time, and it will be wonderful if the temperature stays in the seventies as the days shorten.

Those late October days of 1960 were not very exciting — just calmly satisfying; but one evening we did have a bit of excitement. Just as dusk was approaching we had to call the fire department and ask them to 'come quickly' because there was a fire and we were afraid it was getting out-of-control. Soon the brave men arrived, accompanied by the noisy roar of their engines, and the flames which were threatening to engulf one of our trees were dealt with in an efficient manner. Someone must have put a match to the fallen dried leaves and soon a big tree was well and truly ablaze. Fires are most unpleasant things to experience, or even to witness, and I saw one at quite close quarters a few years before. During the time we lived in Surrey, England (in a little house named Rosecroft), there was a serious fire in a house just across the road, almost next door to the little 'Cottage Hospital'. It was a small dwelling with quite a lot of resultant damage, and I certainly hope I will never be closer to a burning building than I was at that moment. To see pieces of charred furniture being brought out onto the street, and the dejected expressions of the occupants as their few goods were ruined by fire and water, was something one would not wish to repeat. In England, in those days smoke chimneys would often catch alight and they sometimes proved to be veritable death traps. Oh yes, we did have a blaze in our chimney while we lived at Rosecroft, but fortunately and to our great relief it was quickly extinguished.

As November approached winter caught up with us and we had a nice carpet of snow in the grounds of Cedar House. The frost was quite biting to the skin but still the Cat people insisted on going outside, chiefly in the middle of the day because the gradually weakening warmth of the sun made conditions somewhat more pleasant and tolerable. As was natural, Miss Sindhi did not seem to feel the cold and north winds so much as the older felines, Mrs. Fifi and Miss Ku'ei. Sindhi would evade all my efforts, all my attempts, to get her into the house when it was felt we had had enough.

Being young and lithe it was not easy for a middle-aged 'Ma' to catch the elusive creature, but in the end we managed with a compromise (most Ma's, usually give in, in the end, just like all human Mamas): I would promise her a nice tidbit if she would come to me, and eventually she would put on her most charming manner and oblige. These sessions used to bring back to mind another incident, this time involving a big black cat who was so huge that he earned for himself the name of Mammoth. Mammoth had been staying with us overnight because his Family were moving or something, and I was to take him from our apartment to South Kensington, London, where his Family would be waiting.

Well, I took this great big cat down the stairs (it was a converted house and therefore no elevator), and being rather small myself Mammoth would have been capable of carrying me instead. A taxi was waiting by the sidewalk and we began to arrange the seating for the two of us when someone from the house distracted my attention, calling me back to discuss something or other. Suddenly there was a wild yell from the cab driver who was in a panic, and he was telling me, 'Hey Missus, yere cat's runnin' up the road!' Certainly by that time I was in a panic too, even if I did not show it, and fortunately Mammoth was a cat of great common sense who realized my difficult situation and suddenly turned around and began running towards me. I was most thankful for it would have been an unhappy position for me had I lost another person's CREATURE. Fortunately the London taxi drivers are, in the main, a philosophical and pleasant breed of individual, and judging from the remarks of this one he was now finding the whole situation cause for loud laughter. . . .

I do not find it easy to write this part of my narrative because it brings me closer to the time when Sindhi would no longer be with us in her physical body; though she has remained very close to us spiritually, communicating with us frequently during the ensuing years.

The time came when we could no longer ignore the situation — no longer blind ourselves to the truth. Our little Baby Cat, it was realized, was very sick indeed, suffering from damage to her brain which undoubtedly had been caused by a blow she must have received when a kitten and which had resulted in the lack of sight in one of her eyes. So, the time came when this little Cat Person, who had come to mean so much to us, had to make her lonely journey to the Land where she might recover; where she WOULD recover; to the Guv's 'Land of the Golden Light' or, as I like to think of it when I go visiting in my dreams, 'Catland'.

FLIGHT OF THE PUSSYWILLOW

CHAPTER ELEVEN

THOSE who have read the Lobsang Rampa books may wonder how it was that there was never any mention at all of Miss Sindhi, until 'Twilight'; but there was a reason for it. This little girl cat was with us at the time the Guv was writing 'The Rampa Story' and he suggested she be included in this story; but she preferred it otherwise, so in deference to her wishes all reference to our Baby Cat was omitted.

However, circumstances change over the years and now that she is a WELL person, with a balanced outlook, she has no objection to her Ma writing about our experiences together. I am reminded of the 35 mm photographic slides which were taken of the three Cat People sitting on the chesterfield in the living room, accompanied by their Ma.

The Guv was the photographer and he posed the subjects beautifully — two creatures on my lap and Granny Grey- whiskers sitting by my side in her usual dignified French manner.

For a time we suffered a great feeling of loss and real sadness, but then we had to put aside our sorrow and get on, once more, with the process of living. Sindhi, after all, was much better off for she had been a most UN-WELL little person during the greater part of her very short life span; so our loss was definitely her real gain and we just had to find satisfaction in her newly found health and happiness.

We had been in this country a little less than two years and the going had not been easy, many customs and ideas being quite different to those of Ireland and England, which was to be expected in a relatively NEW civilization. We did not quickly adapt to the brashness found in the two border towns in which fate had decreed we should find ourselves for about five years following our arrival. The cost of living (a very topical subject at present) was

FLIGHT OF THE PUSSYWILLOW

much higher than we had been experiencing and, since our income was based on the 'Sterling' factor, it was necessary to practice the strictest economical methods in order to exist. But . . . in spite of the obstacles, we DID have our times of fun and merriment. The Guv and Buttercup, both being quite daring one never could predict what they would be up to next, and frequently I was beset by the greatest apprehension if they seemed to be away rather longer than usual. The Guv, being acutely alert mentally, physically too, especially in an emergency; and Buttercup, ever ready for something different, they undertook ventures which would have been beyond Ma's powers of endurance. We often smile, if not laughing outright, when Buttercup in a serious situation is overcome with laughter herself, and the more desperate the situation the more she sees the humorous side. One day she and the Guv came in dripping with water and Buttercup (like me on occasion) seemed incapable of telling a coherent story. We both seem to have a penchant for seeing the 'funny' side of a serious situation. However, it seemed from what I could gather from the Guv's description that he and Buttercup had been walking on the ice on the creek, which but recently had begun to freeze. Buttercup apparently stepped on a very thinly frozen part and, rather naturally, fell through. Of course the Guv reached out to grasp her hand, but he slipped too (we tease her, saying she pulled him in); so they both 'went under'. Obviously Buttercup saw the amusing side of the situation even while she was experiencing a thorough dunking, and I was given to understand she laughed all the way to the house. I really sympathized with her in her predicament since the same thing has happened to me — much to my embarrassment. Of course the Guv's sense of humor is often calculated to test one's self-control which, on oc- casion, seems to be almost nil as far as those two members of the household are concerned.

A few minutes ago I was telling the Guv what I had just typed, so he displayed an amused smile at the memory, while at the same time remarking: 'Well, you know what

really happened, don't you? It was like this . . .' So he went on to explain how there was stagnant water under the ice where the creek met the Niagara river itself. The fast- flowing water had scoured the underside of the ice, leaving only a thin platform on the surface which, when it was stepped upon, 'snapped like a carrot'. 'I don't think I can write that bit,' I commented. 'Snapped like a carrot does not sound good,' I continued. 'Go ahead' he said, 'that is an apt description and write this too.' So I have a little more comment from the Guv, and it pleases me for now we are quits since I contributed a page or two to Chapter Eleven of 'Twilight', he is reciprocating with a few lines in what will probably be Chapter Eleven of the Sindhi Story. So here are his further remarks . . . 'What is known in the Old Country (England) as Salt Ash Rig, which means "wet behind and no fish", because when people went fishing near Salt Ash Bridge they got wet where I said, but no fish because the river is polluted by dockyard effluvia.' I wanted him to write some more because my piece was longer, but he said 'NO! After fifteen books and all the hullabaloo about the last one — leave me out.' Too bad, I consider, but . . . who knows! . . He may have second thoughts and help me out again when I need to have something explained. I certainly hope so for he is very kind and always ready to assist someone in distress. I must work on it . . . and I am fairly certain that another opportunity will present itself sooner or later; and, if necessary, he knows I will ask him outright for assistance. If I don't ask him he is sure to come along at just the right moment, probably with the remark: 'Well, what have you done now? Are you stuck or something?'

CHAPTER TWELVE

AFTER reading the first part of my story someone suggested my narrative should be written in two or three parts, so this seems as suitable a time as any to make the division. The first part was completed over one month ago, in November, and looking outside one could easily believe that Spring had arrived. Well, Easter will be upon us in around three months so the winter will be a short one for us here in Calgary, the city which was named for 'clear running water'; but whether the meaning still holds good is a matter of opinion . . . Let us not get too far ahead of ourselves for we are not yet out of the Christmas festive season. Actually I am writing this on Christmas Day itself as I ponder on the many delightful greetings I have received, even though there is no celebration of this event in our home. As well as the joy of celebration there often seems to be a lot of sadness as the old year is drawing to a close, giving way to the new.

Today we hear of the devastation of a whole city in Australia where many people and animals have died; others injured; most of the survivors in danger of dire sickness; and nearly all of them left homeless.

From a more personal angle, I have just returned from a funeral parlor after paying my last respects to the memory of a friend's husband, the friend being quite distraught at this particular time.

One cannot feel anything but sadness at witnessing the grief of those who are left to struggle on alone, as best they can, following the 'loss' of a loved one, many people not being able to accept — not believing in anything following this life. It is especially hard for a husband or wife who had led a shared life over many years. An apt illustration for life after death was given to me, and I would like to pass it on — the transition may be likened to the egg and the chicken:

FLIGHT OF THE PUSSYWILLOW

Does a chicken feel dead because it emerged from the egg? Rather is it very much alive. And the butterfly! Does IT feel dead because it emerged from the caterpillar? No, of course not — it too feels very much alive. How does one know that the chicken may not have felt imprisoned while in the egg; likewise the butterfly, waiting to emerge from the caterpillar state. Thus with the human body, or animal either for that matter. To leave the human shell temporarily, even in sleep, can be a wonderful experience, so how much more so to leave permanently. It seems that the greatest difficulty for those who 'pass over' is the grief which the friends and relatives display — those who are left behind. If we think about it, we who are left to mourn are really sorrowing for ourselves, for our own loss, and not for the one who has gone on to far, far greener pastures. Most of us have heard of one person at least who, while experiencing a serious illness, has told of going to some glorious place far more beautiful and more peaceful than anything which could be experienced down here. Especially does this seem to be true of a person who almost drowns, and then recovers — often expressing disappointment that the beautiful experience had to end.

Then one has heard of someone who really did not want to return to their body, and they distinctly remember being told that they must return for their lifespan was not yet finished, and there was still a task to be accomplished or a lesson to be learnt.

Many books seem to have been written recently about the process of dying, and it is becoming accepted more and more that the so-called 'mystery of death' is nothing more than a transitory state, a condition commonly known as a state of transition such as happens in the case of the chicken and the caterpillar.

From a personal angle I can truthfully say that, although my Mother long ago passed to the other side of life, I still often feel her presence very strongly. This feeling is especially strong around Christmas time because, for one thing, she was a very spiritual person and this period meant a very great deal to her. Her strong religious convictions helped her greatly in coping with the many vicissitudes which beset her, not the least of her problems being her somewhat wayward daughter who had been anything but a placid child.

It may be advisable before going any further to mention the reason for my bringing something of my personal, earlier life into this story. This was also suggested to me so, just to show that not all May born people are always obstinate and cussed, and being in one of my more amiable moods, I conceded to this request — or suggestion. So, to return to the matter in question — the problem of death and transition.

In the days subsequent to my Mother's passing I was very unhappy for some time because she meant more to me than any other person. One may have many friends and associates but only One Mother, and I had never been able to envisage life without HER in the background. I often had the impression that she was trying to contact me, trying to give me a message following her 'transition'. It seemed she was trying to impress upon me to go into a certain room where I would not be disturbed and there she would manifest herself before me. Paradoxically, I did not go, even though her message was insistent over a period of some days, and it must have been the cause of much sorrow for her. In those days I had a sort of fear regarding communicating with discarnate beings, so I did not do her bidding for I was apprehensive about coming face-to-face with a ghost. Why should I have been afraid (in death) of some- one who had shown me only love, and the greatest affection in life??? As humans we are most strange, are we not? As a child I was extremely impressionable, and often timid (the aforesaid remark will no doubt cause much amusement in my present household), and it would distress me to walk past a churchyard on a dark night. I would look the other way and hurry past for I was quite sure I would see something unpleasant. When I look back upon those days I wonder how I could have been so foolish, but then I realize that such are the foibles of childhood.

While on the subject of the 'other world', of which most of us still know so little, I am reminded of something which frequently happened to me as a child. In the morning, before actually awakening, I could feel myself spinning, spinning, spinning, like a top; and then finally — bonk, I was lying on my bed — awake and slightly confused. This used to worry me for a long time but now I know that I had been merely returning to my physical body after traveling around in my sleep and I happened to remember, to be aware of the occurrence. But in those days the whole thing was beyond my comprehension. Why am I telling of my own personal experiences instead of keeping to my favorite theme — CATS? Well, as previously stated, it is simply because it was suggested to me and, while I much prefer to live in, and write about the world of cats, especially my own creatures, I can be, on a very rare occasion, sweetly reasonable and prepared to follow another person's advice. I am always prepared to listen to anyone who has a worthwhile suggestion — and the other day a most charming gentleman of my acquaintance commented that he would like to see me writing a book, or books, for children. But to write for children one needs to have a special kind of outlook, and training perhaps; but I gave it a lot of thought and it would make me happy to be able to entertain this segment of society.

From the earliest days I can remember I have always felt that there was a special reason for my existence, for my continuing to keep on living. And I must have exhausted the proverbial nine lives of a cat; each time I have been in danger something prevented the event becoming a tragedy.

It took me quite a long time before I realized my ultimate purpose, but now I am aware of it I am trying my best to fulfill my 'behind-the-scenes' task.

But let us get back to Christmas — the time for children, and for remembering — and for the Family life of Childhood. Hanging up one's stocking by the chimney (in a REAL house instead of an apartment), waking up in the middle of the night wondering if 'He' had been, and not daring to make a sound lest one disturbed 'Him'. Santa Claus was a very REAL PERSON.

My Mother used to tell me about a little girl whose name was Topsy, and 'Santa Claus' visit to 'Topsy' is still imprinted on my consciousness:

'Through the loneliest hours of the night she watched

For she knew the Saint would come

Because right up from her childhood days

He never had missed her home.

But some of the girls at school had said,

Had said it again and again

That there really was no Santa Claus

And as Topsy was only ten

And the wisdom of ten was not very wise

And the girls who said it were tall

Our poor little Topsy had blinked her eyes

FLIGHT OF THE PUSSYWILLOW

Til the tears began to fall . . .'

This little rhyme, the origin of which I am unaware, was of such interest that it has stayed clearly in my mind, along with many other thoughts of a good and loving Mother whose only fault may have lain in her leniency towards her strong-willed, and sometimes hot tempered, daughter. But the example she showed would far outweigh any minor defects from which she may have suffered. A person who sees only the best in all other humans, always making allowances for them, must in my book of values have attained some degree of enlightenment.

Ah, yes, I still believe in Santa Claus.

CHAPTER THIRTEEN

SOMEONE once said, 'It is not what we fear but what we desire that is most dangerous.' Surely that remark contains a great deal of truth for our desires are often exactly the opposite of what is good for us. Our fears often prove to be groundless, but our desires are something else again—

The other day I read an extract which shows that a fear, or apprehension of the unknown, is not uncommon. The piece went like this: A mother said to her child, 'If at night you see a ghost, or in the cemetery you see apparitions who threaten you, don't be afraid. Be brave and attack them; then they will run away.' The child considered the remark for a moment and then came back with, 'What if their mother has given them the same advice?' I thought this quite amusing, though very sensible from the child's point of view, and quite worth recording here since it fits in with my story.

When I was quite young I used to hear the older people discussing what they termed 'White Brothers' and apparently these discarnate figures could be seen quite clearly by certain people. A true experience was related by a man who was traveling on horseback through dangerous terrain. Suddenly a group of bandits were about to leap towards him, ostensibly to rob him and cause him bodily harm, when just as suddenly they drew back, nervous and afraid, with ashen faces, and disappeared. The man who had been traveling on horseback related that during the journey he had been accompanied by two figures, one on each side of him, and both of them riding horses. The white-robed figures were so solid as to be easily seen by the traveler — and apparently by the bandits also, hence their fright; thus the traveler was protected while he completed his mission. Being of a very imaginative nature, I would listen in awe about the society of the 'White Brotherhood'. Fortunately these happenings were accepted in my home, thus I had no trouble in accepting the unusual experiences which confronted me later in my own life.

You have heard people say, 'I have never seen a ghost. I have never seen anything unusual . . . Why don't I see some of the things I hear about?' . . . 'Other people see things but it seems that such experiences are not for me.'

How do we know whether or not we have seen a ghost which is merely an extension of a person, detached and manifesting some distance away from the physical body.

You will find a person deploring the fact that they 'never see anything such as a flying saucer', and wondering why other people have all the luck. How do we know whether or not we have witnessed the sighting of a U.F.O.? Unless we are well acquainted with astronomy we cannot be sure that a 'star' in the sky is not an unidentified flying object. It has been my satisfying experience to witness some of these apparently unusual phenomena through a quite powerful telescope and anyone who has had such an opportunity as this would hardly be likely to disbelieve the fact of their existence. The magnified colors and shapes are a really wonderful, never-to-be forgotten sight. But I am not sufficiently informed, or experienced, to have a discussion regarding the pros and cons of U.F.O.'s, so I will leave this subject to those who are more enlightened on the matter — those who have really made a study of it.

I will stay with ghosts . . . which seem to be more my forte.

Some years ago I had a very interesting experience while living in the suburbs of London. I was standing on the platform at South Kensington waiting for the train which would soon be arriving, and which would take me the journey of twenty minutes or so to my home in Surrey. Just idly watching the other passengers and wondering who they were and where they might be going, what kind of jobs they might have, etcetera, I saw an acquaintance, standing nearby, with whom I had recently been chatting in an office. I was a little surprised to see her going home so early as she had not appeared ready to leave when I had left. As the approaching train pulled up, stopping before us, we entered at the same time, and sat down together — immediately becoming engaged in conversation. The young lady seemed to be rather quiet; but she looked more full of color, more radiant, than she had seemed on other occasions. She was carrying a purse (or handbag) and a larger bag containing her office needs and the like, and these items attracted my attention — my eyes being riveted on their brightness. The colors of the large bag, especially, were quite vivid and seemed to be surrounded by a 'special' glow. The meaning I am trying to convey is one of extreme brightness, not actually more colorful but really GLOWING. We were not sufficiently closely acquainted to be talking about anything very serious or intimate, merely carrying on a light conversation — probably both wishing the journey was over so that we could quickly reach our respective homes. I had a beautiful silver tabby cat waiting for me, and I knew he would be anxiously awaiting my arrival; and he would be ready for supper so, after alighting from the train we sauntered out of the station and onto the street. I believe I asked her whether she was going my way; but apparently she wasn't — and she simply drifted away. Later that evening I mentioned the event to the third person who had been in the office that afternoon and how I had traveled with Miss Secretary. You can picture my surprise when I was told, 'You could not possibly have traveled with her for she was still in the office talking to me.'

What was it? An unsolved mystery? Not at all! Miss Secretary was merely thinking very strongly about her own affairs, and wanting to leave early, and she had used so much thought power in the effort that she had made a 'form' and actually traveled out to the suburbs in such solid form that she could be seen. This is not a rare occurrence for I have read and heard of many similar instances; so I do not find it strange — but just something of extreme interest. The same very bright light was visible when my Silver Tabby was preparing to make his final farewell and getting ready to return to his heavenly home, and caused (I believe) by unseen entities who came to assist in his passing.

Another time I was sitting in a bus in the Maida Vale district of London. It was raining quite heavily and the bus stopped to allow passengers to enter or leave the vehicle. I was indulging in a bit of daydreaming, as usual, when suddenly I came back into focus at the sight of a young, attractive woman just entering the vehicle. She was fair-haired and wore an attractive head-dress, and a coat light in color.

It seemed most strange that, although there was a real downpour at that time, this young person was completely dry — as dry as if she had stepped right out of a beauty parlor; and this surprised me! also the fact that she seemed to be enveloped in a 'brightness', which was missing as far as the other passengers were concerned.

CHAPTER FOURTEEN

NEW YEAR — 1975: A brand new year and already just over one week has passed. In the light of experiences and events it feels more like several weeks, and it is nice just to sit down and record some of these happenings which are now history. Over and over again the thought comes to mind that really today is the only day which matters — having done one's best in each situation one can look back with satisfaction, and forward with anticipation to what one hopes will be even greater achievements tomorrow, which all too soon will be today.

Look to this day!

For it is life, the very life of life . . .

For yesterday is already a dream,

and tomorrow is only a vision;

But today, well lived, makes every yesterday

A dream of happiness, and every tomorrow

a vision of hope.

From the Sanskrit

With the New Year winter has really arrived in Calgary, although Winnipeg is having a much worse time; but the zero and sub-zero temperatures, with snow and strong winds which we are experiencing, are just enough for me as I get bundled up in warm clothing each morning at eight-thirty in preparation for a walk to the post office to collect our mail — a walk which I really enjoy. Today the local newspaper comments that 'Those who have been THINKING "snow" will be rewarded, even if the price they pay will be bone-chilling temperatures.' Unwittingly perhaps, the writer admits that Thought is Real, a form of energy which has the power to make things happen. This is encouraging for too often events are looked upon as 'coincidence'. So, if the newspaper makes such a statement, why gosh, it must be true.

How many people just seem to act without much thought, expecting all good things will come to them without any effort on their part — not realizing that things happen only when we plan them first in our minds. We have to devote a great deal of thought power in our lives, otherwise we are no more, or less, than vegetables; and it has often been said that 'we are what we think we are'. If we think confidence, we radiate confidence, and others will believe in us; but if we are timid, undecided and changeable, we transmit this atmosphere to those around us, leaving worth cultivating.

The past ten days have been full of activity and of planning; full of action which has brought some quite satisfactory results, including new acquaintances with like interests to my own.

On Christmas Day I had paid my first visit to a Funeral Home and witnessed the sadness of an acquaintance whose husband had passed away. Just one week later I was asked to assist in another case of sickness - this time a beautiful Siamese Mother Cat. Nikki, a delightful Blue Point, had been sick for some months and it had been decided that the time had arrived when her discomfort and pain should come to an end, and she should be allowed to go Home. The person with whom Nikki had lived for around twelve years was under great emotional stress, and she said she would appreciate some assistance during this trying time. So, a comfortable carrying basket was prepared for this delicate little creature and I went along to Shirley's house where she was waiting with Mother Cat Nikki. All arrangements had been made and we drove carefully to the Pet Hospital (the Westside Hospital of course) where we were received with quiet understanding. Having passed the basket over to Dr. R., the veterinarian, we stayed until Nikki had quietly and peacefully passed on, to her Real Home, after which we made our way back to our own Unreal homes — our temporary earth abodes. In spite of the loss and accompanying sadness, we were left with a warm feeling of achievement knowing that Nikki, the little Mother Cat, would have no more pain and discomfort from the tumors which had caused her to suffer the trauma of surgery on several occasions; tumors which had probably been caused through the consumption of too many 'pills' when she was 'calling' and a delay of several years before spaying, and then only because the authorities decided the pills could be harmful.

At home Shirley has two male Seal Point Siamese, both of them of a quite mature age. One, Nikki's son Ichabod — aged ten years, and a Grampa Cat of sixteen years but who gives the impression of being very much younger. He carries his years very well, with dignity, and I was honored to meet this Cat Family, who were most polite when I visited them in their home. And I have been invited to call upon them whenever I find it convenient — which I wish could be more often.

If I were to give a title to the past week or so — the first days of 1975, it would just have to be 'Feline Affairs' week.

On the first day of the year a man asked me if I knew someone who would take his two Siamese cats because his landlord was making his life difficult, not wanting him to have pets in his house. Tiki and Shara, two Gentlemen Cats, were around one year old, he told me. They were Seal Point and very healthy, but if something could not be done very quickly they would have to be sent off to the S.P.C.A.

Well, I had to make a number of telephone calls, and I spoke to a number of acquaintances about the situation — and came across quite a number of obstacles: Some people were interested but wanted only one cat; some wanted younger cats; others wanted this, and others that. I could not bear to think of these two young cats being sent to the S.P.C.A., and the possibility of them being 'put to sleep' was something not to be contemplated. Something just had to be done! But what?

After much negotiating, and temporary arrangements made for the future, Shirley went with me to collect these two fine specimens, Tiki and Shara, and helped me convey them to the veterinary hospital for a check-up, etcetera. They were to have their annual distemper and rabies' shots, and were to be neutered since that is most essential for tom cats who are going to be so-called 'pets'. As we arrived at their house (a few minutes late since we almost got lost finding the place) they were waiting for us, and while driving to the Pet Hospital they displayed near-perfect manners; and they were no trouble at all. I have been given to under- stand they had received a good European disciplinary training, and everybody at the Pet Hospital was really excited at the sight of them, with their dark seal coloring. Shirley was very interested in a big female Siamese sitting in a big cage and waiting to be shipped to Toronto, most likely by air, where the Family were moving to a new home. Tiki and Shara had shared their home with three teenaged girls who would certainly miss their pets; and one was left with a feeling of sadness at the apparent uncaring attitude of a Landlord who would cause the disruption of two young feline lives, a disorientation which could take a long time to rectify.

Shara and Tiki are now in a temporary home (which may prove to be permanent), with understanding persons, a mother and daughter, who are quite intrigued with these two boy cats — although they already have a Family of Felines — and on the two occasions when I have visited them, Tiki and Shara greeted me enthusiastically.

So, the first days of January kept me so busy that there was no time to record the experiences until now.

But it is a nice time of the year for a number of reasons — one of the most important is the bringing together of friends, old and new; those who for one reason or another think about us but never seem to get down to communicating — other than by telepathy, which can at times have as much effect as a letter. Such a person— is Gertrude Lavery, who lives in Australia, and she has corresponded with me for about a decade — or just a little less. Mrs. Lavery is of German origin and at one time we communicated via a tape recorder, but sickness and other commitments have intervened and now we manage quite well with about two letters a year — at Christmas and halfway through the year (on our respective birthdays). This interesting person, with whom I have ex- changed many thoughts, many ideas and experiences, now lives in West Perth. She is very satisfied with her small apartment, and Mr. and Mrs. Hyde (who own the building) have been most kind and helpful — providing the greatest assistance during Mrs. Lavery's difficult period of ill health.

And their Siamese cat, Cindy, often visits her and enjoys sitting on her lap while she reads and writes letters. Apparently Cindy is a very good Watch-Cat, and she won't allow any other felines into the yard. She has been known to terrify creatures who infringe on her territory, while they have to take refuge on the limb of a tree. Mrs. Lavery has given me permission to mention her in this story, even suggested it, and I am very happy to do just that as I was to receive last week her first letter of 1975. Mrs. Lavery has kept in touch through the years and her encouraging letters have cheered us in some of our darker moments.

FLIGHT OF THE PUSSYWILLOW

Yes, we have had more than our share of 'dark moments', and this is one reason I want to keep my story light — to remember the pleasant times.

While on the subject of Australia I am reminded of another delightful person, who wrote several letters to us around the time that we first heard from Mrs. Lavery. This person was also living in Australia and I remember her particularly for the sympathy she showed at the time of the Lady Ku-ei's last illness, which was caused by the harassment of the media, and I will always remember how she finished one of her letters, with the following words:

'Why do they (the Press) judge so harshly that which they do not understand — for judge you harshly they have.'

She was referring not only to the Press but also to various individuals who, through jealousy and envy, had taken great pains to egg them on.

Many times have I felt a glow of gratitude towards this English person who was at that time living in Australia, and often I have regretted losing contact with her — she who was there at just the right moment.

FLIGHT OF THE PUSSYWILLOW

CHAPTER FIFI'EEN

THIS will be the third part of my story; a true story by the way, and perhaps the pleasantest to record for I am going to tell of our two present Felines — our Cat People of TODAY; not yesterday, but of THIS DAY, and tomorrow, which soon will be today.

At this stage, here in Calgary my personal private life leaves nothing to be desired, but at the same time there is more than a tinge of sadness — in the fact of the Guv's extreme sickness and the pain which he suffers at all times. We are often told, and we read too, that a certain amount of tension and stress is necessary for an individual to survive, to make progress, and that without this 'tension' we would be in danger of collapsing. Well, in my opinion and in the opinion of many others, Lobsang Rampa has suffered far more than should be expected of anyone; and much of the suffering could have been avoided if certain persons had attended to their own affairs instead of meddling in other people's business. It is very true that the more a person is working for the good of others, the more the obstacles appear and evil influences seem to fight for superiority.

Only this morning I heard from England that all kinds of people are putting out all kinds of stories; first time authors are going along with the news media and cashing in on what they have persuaded themselves is a bit of sensation, a bit of scandal, thereby hoping to secure for themselves a bit of temporary fame. I had not intended to introduce any of this into my story but I have been so disgusted at the things I have heard that my conscience tells me if I did not utter a word of protest I might just as well be condoning the acts of those who 'write' saying Lobsang Rampa is a phony — a fake. It cannot be reiterated too often that his books are absolutely true; they are all his own experiences, and he and his works are accepted by enlightened Tibetans; the present Dalai Lama on occasion sending him encouraging messages, the latest being a few weeks ago through a mutual acquaintance in the United States of America. The severest of his critics must agree that he has something; it shows by the number of his books which have been sold and the number of persons who have been helped through them.

These facts speak for themselves. It has been pointed out to us quite often that those who make the biggest noise are those who have never read the Rampa books and have no idea what they are about. It makes me sad that so much of this criticism originates in England, a country which the rest of the world has so long looked upon as an example of right thinking and right living. A certain section of the British, in spite of their apparent aloofness and fair-play attitude, are inclined to revel in sensational stories — not necessarily accurate, and more often than not anything but — I should know, having spent a good part of my life on that little island, and learned from experience. Some of the newspapers, especially the Sunday issues, can be really hair-raising, and once they get hold of a subject they tend to adopt a 'flog a dead horse' attitude; and the great reading public (the number is obvious if one checks on the number of copies sold), which consists of the greater part of the population, enjoys it 'to the death'.

When I lived in Ireland a British pressman told me that truth and accuracy are secondary in importance when reporting — what really matters is the sensational value, whether it results in sickness, or even suicide, for the victim.

The Pressman must have his story even if he has to 'fiction- alize.' Probably small countries suffer from this much more than the larger areas of the world where, one hopes, the people have bigger minds and give the individual a chance to vindicate himself. An Englishman, Mr. Cyrus Brooks, once volunteered the remark, when we had commented upon the adverse and unwarranted publicity we were receiving, 'Oh well, an author stands up to be shot at.' Well, it is the opinion of many people that Lobsang Rampa has received more than his share of shotgun blasts — mainly caused through hate and spite.

Some years ago we contemplated living on a much smaller island even, the smallest island in the English Channel. We were in communication with the late Sybil Hathaway, the Dame of Sark, who ruled over that little island.

There was an accommodation problem so the idea fell through, but I often thought it would have been nice to live in a place away from automobiles, buses, and all power-drawn vehicles such as Sark island offered. On the other hand, I wonder whether we would have found the peace we were looking for, in a community that was little more than a village. Perhaps this is one of the reasons I enjoy Calgary, for here no one bothers us — we are left to live out our lives in whichever way suits us best. The people here must be amongst the most friendly in all of this large contingent, and it is interesting to see their smile of appreciation when they realize that one is a Canadian Citizen.

Cleo and Taddy, the Seal Point and Blue Point Siamese people are Canadian-born, of course, and they are futuristic felines, being born in the Constellation of Aquarius. Since they will be celebrating their respective birthdays towards the end of this month, it seems a most appropriate time to bring them into my story. They have brought much joy into this household, and we have a lot of fun together. Cleo, the little one (scraggy by Taddy's standards), is the most understanding Cat Person we have met. And Taddy, the big Fat Cat, need's a great deal of my attention and encouragement, not being quite so self-confident as her sister. I must point out that of course these two are the Guv's cats as well as mine but, really, it might be more accurate to look upon ourselves as 'their cats'. Cleo has a delightful sense of humor, and to see her put her little face up close to the Guv's ear and blow into his hearing aid is quite an amusing sight, as when she is sitting somewhere on high and reaches down to give me a light touch with her paw, being careful not to bonk me too hard, for I understand she would not like to upset her Ma who I am proud to say she holds in high regard.

These two Cat Persons are as well-behaved as any creatures I have ever met, and probably better behaved than most. Just to show how well, I must relate the following —

On these January nights, with their lower temperatures, I sometimes feel the cold in my bones, and since my bedroom faces North it never gets warmth from the sun. Therefore, I use an electric pad which warms the bed before I retire, and does the same should I wake up feeling chilly during the night.

Cleo often sits on the pad (which is covered by a sheet and a blanket) a little while before bed-time, and occasionally she drops off to sleep while she waits for me. The moment I am ready for bed myself this little cat will come sufficiently awake to trundle off to her own bed, sometimes shooting off like a bird, where she and Taddy have a hot water bottle to keep them warm.

This delightful gesture of Cleo's really impresses me — her supreme consideration for others; but that seems to be her whole attitude to life — to cause as little trouble as possible, and to help others whenever she can.

Taddy has a slightly different approach to life, believing herself to be a rather grumpy old biddy; but her Ma holds a rather different opinion of the Big Fat Cat who weighs around twice as much as her sister, Cleopatra. Taddy would be the first to agree that Taddy's main interest in life is FOOD, and I understand she believes herself to be UNDER FED also.

Sometimes when I am reading in bed or listening to the radio, Fat Cat will come and plonk herself beside me, resting her paws on my arm so that I am unable to move, and there she will stay for perhaps half-an-hour; then she will go off to visit the Guv and check to see if adequate food has been left out for the night — 'for the cats'. A little later she returns and decides to relax a little by sitting on the pillow behind my head, arms folded and a look of bliss upon her sweet face.

The other day someone gave me a tape recording from the Jonathan Livingston Seagull film, so the three of us have been spending many enjoyable moments imagining we are sky-birds flying high with Jonathan Seagull, who had that beautiful story written about him.

Cleo and Taddy take their duties very seriously and many times each night they wander off to visit the Guv, trying to cheer him and hoping to ease his pain with their purrs of affection, showing him how they care about his well-being.

They have been known to take turns 'on duty', and when the Guv is more sick than usual they are very concerned indeed. During the past two nights Miss Taddy has been putting in extra hours because she has been very worried lest the Guv was about to leave us. Oh yes, Taddy puts on an apparently gruff exterior but, in reality, she is possessed of a really nice and kind nature; and she is aided greatly by a most devoted and intelligent Cleo Cat. I understand Taddy is very proud of her knowledgeable sister, of the graceful curves and agile movements, and that when she refers to the 'skinny cat' she is merely making the remark in fun.

CHAPTER SIXTEEN

THERE must be no greater lovers of riding in an automobile than Siamese cats. Perhaps other types enjoy it too, but most of my experience has been with Siamese, and they were all fascinated with it. Fifi Greywhiskers was an exception, but she had traveled around so much in unhappy circumstances and conditions that, in the end, HOME was all she wanted. The Silver Tabby (of pre-Ku'ei days) objected most strongly when taken into a small Morris Minor car.

Yesterday we went for a drive towards the foothills, it being in the form of a celebration birthday party for Cleo and Taddy — for where would you find a S'mese inviting other S'meses, or any other kind of cat, to visit them. So — a drive seemed appropriate and we enjoyed it immensely.

It was the first time I had viewed the city from such a height and the atmosphere was so pollution-free that we could see everything in detail, from the television building on the Hill to the Calgary Tower (the mainland mark was clearly visible), as well as the many high-rise apartment buildings — one of which is our temporary home.

Cleo enjoyed herself by sitting on the rear window, arms folded, and looking into the car; while Taddy 'hiked' around under and over the seats, muttering occasionally when she stubbed a toe.

Many drivers and their passengers showed interest in the Little Cat, and as we would pause at intersections she was pointed out a number of times.

On the way home we called to see Tiki and Shara, and Mrs. Potter who looks after them, along with the other felines. At present she has a litter of Siamese kittens, and they all yelled together — then purred, putting their paws out in greeting (Siamese cats are very polite if you treat them civilly, as intelligent persons). Of course I left Cleo and Taddy in the car with the driver and went into the house alone. Mrs. Potter cares for a number of cats, of different types, and her so-called 'Cattery' is one of the happiest places and best appointed I have ever heard of. The big 'cages' are two-floor affairs, and the inhabitants use a ladder covered with carpeting to ascend or descend from one floor to another. Tiki and Shara have settled down extremely well and it is quite likely that Mrs. Potter will adopt them permanently.

During the past few days, and seeing how Cleo and Taddy have become such beautiful creatures, I have been reminded of the time they first arrived into our household. Poor Little People! Rather undersized and somewhat afraid, I had brought them to Fort Erie from Niagara Falls one Sunday morning. Two weeks earlier I had gone to see these Little People with their sisters and brothers, and it had been my responsibility to choose them. We had already decided upon the Blue Point, who we were later to name Tadalinka; so I had to choose another creature to accompany her. I was told that the Little Cleopatra (who was named already) had near-perfect markings for a Seal Point and that I could take her if I wished, otherwise she would be kept for breeding purposes. So the matter was settled. But the Little People were two weeks short of being able to leave their Cat Mother and therefore arrangements were made to return for them two weeks later, and I was given to understand that those two stayed close together during the whole of the waiting period.

After the departure of Miss Ku'ei it had not occurred to me to consider having any more cats because the situation was quite unsettled as far as our movements were concerned we were not sure where we were going to be living.

Another problem was the frequent ban on having a pet in an apartment complex, and this was a cause of much concern. We were to have more problems in this respect a few years later when we moved to Western Canada where, in British Columbia (Vancouver and Victoria, on the Island particularly), there is an almost total ban on having a pet. You could not be much worse off if you had the plague — you make a few inquiries and call upon one Superintendent after another and are offered a nice comfortable place, situated fairly high, with an attractive view, and within the price range you have set for yourself. Then, 'Come along, Ma'am, I will take you up in the elevator and I am sure you will not be disappointed.' I accompany Mr. Superintendent and we chat amiably, each of us weighing up the other; and we view the premises together; and then I am ready to discuss the project in more detail. Eventually, and before getting too involved, I casually mention my two well-behaved little Lady Cats. And then comes the bombshell: 'Sorry, Ma'am, no pets allowed by order of the Company. It is Company policy.' The atmosphere has changed and Mr Superintendent suddenly finds he has many things awaiting his attention and he cannot get away fast enough. It was for this reason that we found ourselves in Calgary, where Cleo and Taddy are more than welcome in our present home; but I understand that even in this city it is sometimes a bit difficult getting settled into accommodation if you have a Cleo or a Taddy. Just before leaving Vancouver we were attracted to a desirable location which offered a Penthouse, with a good view of the sea; so we experienced a short period of hopefulness. This time it was the janitor's wife who showed me around, and she was most friendly and anxious to have us because she said they were tired of renting to younger persons with 'their noisy parties and rock'n roll mentality, and all that goes with it'. Especially did they need quiet tenants because the people in the adjoining Penthouse were rather important; they had been there for sometime and already there had been some annoyance through previous fellow tenants causing a disturbance on the communicating patios.

'You are just the type of people we want,' said Mrs. Caretaker 'who don't make too much noise and so cause less trouble for us.' 'That's just fine,' I answered 'but you know we have two "pets", two Siamese Ladies,' and I observed her reactions as I made the announcement. She made no secret of the fact that in her mind we would be a most desirable family to have in her building, so I was counting on it rather strongly. After giving the matter a few seconds consideration she suggested we just take the cats into the apartment as quietly as possible, not mentioning about them to anyone, assuming that once inside they would never need to be taken out until we were leaving the place. What to do about the patio was not mentioned, and I imagined the scene if Cleo and Taddy were to wander into the neighbors' quarters, unannounced, when cats were not even allowed into the building.

Apparently the Rental Manager, who was off duty (otherwise he would have interviewed me), was not in a position to allow pets so Mrs. Janitor warned me not to mention anything about it to him when we would sign the lease; so I told her I would have to discuss the matter with the other members of my Family and then I would contact her again.

Naturally the Guv would not agree to such an arrangement. He would not

FLIGHT OF THE PUSSYWILLOW

take his Cat Children 'though the back door'. They would enter openly with us or we would give up the idea altogether, which we did; and, as I mentioned, that was one of the reasons we took off for Calgary, which proved to be somewhat more humanitarian — or should it be 'humane'?

Oh dear, there I go digressing again! But now let us return and pick up the loose threads which we left in Fort Erie. Following the time that Sindhi had left us we had been beset by many difficulties, which finally resulted in our making a journey to South America where we hoped things would improve. While the trip was most educational it proved to be anything but a happy period. Certainly the climate of Uruguay was pleasant, without extremes of temperature, so it was fortunate that by the time we set foot in Canada again Spring was already with us.

During that summer in Fort Erie, Miss Ku'ei and I spent many moments strolling along the street outside the small dwelling where we were living. Mrs. Fifi Greywhiskers had passed on some time before, thus Ku'ei felt a great sense of loss; and this loneliness for her adopted sister brought us closer together, but often when we were enjoying our walks in the warm sunshine I felt an urge to provide for her as much companionship as possible because I had a feeling, a premonition if you like, that it would probably be the last summer we would spend together; which, unhappily, proved correct.

She struggled through the following Fall and Winter months, and the following Spring, as the days began to lengthen she seemed to be a little brighter — to be improving a little. Naturally I was very happy about this; but my joy was short-lived for, suddenly, sadness tinged our lives once again, with disastrous results for my Ku'ei Cat.

A Press reporter arrived from the local newspaper to tell us about an incident which had occurred in England and he wanted to see what we had to say about it. A young man had committed suicide, and while that in itself was not uncommon, it seemed that one of Lobsang Rampa's books had been found in the young man's room, along with works by other writers no doubt, but apparently none so well-known as the Guv; therefore not so newsworthy.

Just tailor-made for the Press though, and with a fair amount of encouragement from one or two private persons who considered they had 'an axe to grind', the affair was blown up out of all proportion to the actual facts.

74

FLIGHT OF THE PUSSYWILLOW

Fortunately, having been forewarned, we were not too surprised or startled when, towards the evening of the same day, another Pressman appeared at our door. Oh, yes, he was a middle-aged individual who appeared full of concern for us, being quick to accept our hospitality and, on the surface, a typical friendly Canadian.

The story he told was that he had been to the Niagara Falls area 'on a case' and as he was driving along, preparing for the return journey to Toronto, he had received a tele- phone message in his car. He said his Head Office had told him there was a news item in the offing and, since he was in the area, he may as well call and investigate it. All very casual on the surface. Apparently he had shown little interest in the project, which anyway was going to delay his arrival home in Toronto, until he suddenly realized it was something to do with the author of 'The Third Eye' which was causing the interest; so then, he said he was 'turned on'.

It was after that interview at Fort Erie that I vowed I would never again cooperate with a newspaper man or woman, after the way this one accepted our hospitality professing friendship and understanding of the situation and leaving with a promise of sympathetic coverage, together with a book by the author which he said he was sure he would enjoy reading. The next day we were greeted with a report which we might never have recognized except for one or two remarks, and the author's autographed volume having been included in the 'copy' with the caption, 'The Murder Book'.

Yes, apparently a nice family man, brimming over with sympathy and understanding — returning again two days later to complete his investigation, but not receiving such a friendly reception — and there disappeared any confidence I might ever have felt towards ANY news reporter.

Miss Ku'ei, having seen this type of thing happen again and again during her comparatively long life, just gave up and her condition rapidly deteriorated until she could no longer withstand the lies and deceit, the treachery and misrepresentation of the facts — man's inhumanity to man which to so-called 'dumb animals' is beyond comprehension — and so she left us.

Was it coincidence I wonder that, before too long, that particular newspaper left us also. It ceased publication and is no longer in circulation—

Anyway, I have often given a thought to that particular reporter — without admiration. Ours was not an isolated case of harassment and from what one learns the situation is not getting any better. Just today I read a comment by Lauren Bacall, the screen and stage star who surely has led an exemplary life, and there seems no reason that she should be maligned by the media.

Like many of us she has suffered many difficulties and set- backs not of her own making; and she was a great help to her husband, Humphrey Bogart, during the critical days of his terminal illness.

Regarding the Press, she has this to say: 'Probably the most infuriating things are the lies they tell about you. I don't understand why people make up such stories. Does it make them feel important?' (McCall's — February 1975). With Miss Bacall, many of us are left with no answer unless it is that newspapers sell in greater number if they concentrate on SENSATION and FICTION, rather than the TRUTH.

CHAPTER SEVENTEEN

How often have I proved the truth of the saying that 'every cloud has its silver lining'. Just when everything appears at its blackest, there, on the horizon, glows a ray of sunshine and hope.

Suddenly we were confronted with an unpleasant situation, although the whole affair had really been nothing at all to do with us, and this situation led to the loss of my dearest companion, The Lady Ku'ei.

I grieved for myself. I was very lonely without her company, though she was much better off having gone to join Mrs. Fifi Greywhiskers and Miss Sindhi, and all the others who were there waiting for her to return Home.

Showing a selfish attitude I did not enjoy being left alone and I did not want to experience such a situation again. I reasoned that if I did decide to have another creature, inevitably I would have to repeat this experience one day — assuming I lived that long. The next one would leave and once more I would be overcome with grief. Then, as the picture became a little clearer, and feeling a little less selfish for a moment, I thought: 'Supposing MY life-span should prove to be shorter than that of another Cat Person! What would become of the creature who by then would have become used to MY ways and the ways of MY household?'

Eventually, after much thought and discussion with the Family, I saw that perhaps all these obstacles may only be excuses and that here was another opportunity for helping Cat People who need to get their earth experience just as we humans do, otherwise they would not be placed down here.

If I could help to make life easier, even for one of them, then surely it would be worthwhile. So eventually I decided to go ahead with plans for finding a Little Person. And my search ended when I met those two, Cleopatra the Seal Point Siamese, and Tadalinka the Blue Point Siamese, and they provided the silver lining to the dark clouds. This was just what we needed, but once more our peace had been disturbed and again our lives were not our own.

Various reporters, fiction, or rather 'feature' writers, whose work might at times appear more fictional than fact, kept appearing at our door, all wanting to tell a story, and life was becoming quite unbearable for us.

Again we had to review the situation, and it was obvious we would have to consider making a further move, something not one of us was happy about since we had barely settled down following our South American experience. To those who say, 'It must be wonderful moving around all the time, seeing fresh places and getting to know different people', I would tell them: 'Don't you believe it, for unless you are absolutely compelled to do so the time taken in physical and mental energy, the cost of moving, and the things which get 'lost' or damaged in transit, added to the problem of arranging a new home (an accommodation address in our case, which is usually a post office box), and making oneselves known to the business people, etcetera, can leave one quite exhausted.' You might ask, 'Why a P.O. Box. Can't you have your mail sent to your home? Why run around making extra work for yourselves when the mailman will go to your door?' To that I can only say that it does not work because we have tried it. When we lived in the Montreal area we thought we would take a chance and use our private address, which we did to our regret. People would just wander around the grounds of Habitat and look for us, especially on Sunday afternoons. They wanted to meet Lobsang Rampa, the well-known author, and they thought it was just a matter of asking and they would have immediate access to him; and of course they were quite surprised and disappointed when they had to leave without seeing him. One amusing experience comes to my mind, and this was a case of two young readers of the Guv's books. One day when he was out these two arrived at the door; they were quite pleasant and well-mannered and, I believe, they were just temporary visitors to Montreal, having traveled from the U.S.A. It is not easy to deter young people these days; they wanted to sit on the steps outside to await the return of Lobsang Rampa — the object of their visit. At last I persuaded them that it would be foolish to wait since their presence would not be exactly welcome; but not before they spied a pair of shoes just inside the door, exclaiming, "Tell us, are those his shoes." As they walked away, looking quite disappointed, I felt sorry for their wasted journey.

FLIGHT OF THE PUSSYWILLOW

Well it was a good thing all was quiet when the Guv returned because he gave me to understand that I had done well to shoo away the visitors because they would not have been at all welcome. Still, I knew just how they felt, and later they wrote a nice letter of apology for disturbing us.

As will often happen in life, something good comes along just when we seem to have come up against a blank wall, and this was one of those times. Knowing that if we were to stay on in Fort Erie, especially in the same accommodation (and there was little choice, for rented houses or apartments were at a premium in those days), we could not expect to be left alone. We felt it was essential to make other arrangements, and quickly.

But what could we do! In which direction might we turn Feeling less than cheerful, I went around to the Post Office to buy some stamps and post some packages, and while I waited my turn at the counter I heard a voice behind me which seemed familiar. I turned around to see who it was and there stood a young matron who I had not seen for quite a while. I felt a bit more cheerful while chatting with Lillian who always had an encouraging attitude to life. We talked for a few minutes and then I happened to mention that we contemplated having a change moving to a fresh location, and to my surprise she was able to make a suggestion. It seemed she had contacts about three hundred miles away — far up the St. Lawrence River, near the city of Brockville, and still in Ontario. She gave me an address and a telephone number, so after a quick 'thank you' and a quicker 'good-bye', I hurried home with the good news. At last it seemed that we may have found a place which would suit us, temporarily at least, and I personally felt that so-called 'fate' had not deserted us.

Fate! Or an interested entity! I am inclined to believe the latter for, while Lillian and I were together talking, I had the strongest impression of Miss Ku'ei. It seemed that SHE was responsible for arranging that meeting in the Post Office, and during all the intervening years I have continued to believe it was so. Miss Ku'ei and Lillian had saved the day for us and we were to enjoy a period of peace and calm during the ensuing months.

It must be quite difficult to arrange things down on our materialistic earth, where we hardly dare allow ourselves to believe, or contemplate, anything which we cannot see or prove.

It has been explained by the Guv that one can liken it to the act of trying to put a phonograph needle on a certain part of a disc, hoping to touch the right place. To arrange for two persons to be at the same place at the same time can prove quite a feat — the rate of vibration of a discarnate entity is much more rapid than ours on the earth plane and it is not exactly a simple matter to just make something happen at a certain time.

So many happenings are attributed to so-called CHANCE, coincidence, or blind fate. But if our senses were a bit more 'alert' we would realize that most things are planned.

Of course we have free choice in our actions, within certain limits, but it is how we think and how we act that deter- mines what happens to us. This I know from absolute personal experience, for if I were feeling dispirited and gloomy everything would go wrong and the atmosphere would be radiated to those with whom I might come into contact — to those around me. On the other hand, when I have felt cheerful, contented and happy, everything would go right. If I went on a shopping expedition the articles I bought would be harmonious and satisfactory, while an unhappy mood would produce the most terrible results — wrong colors and wrong styles in the way of clothes or furnishing for the home. One particular time, I was having new eye-glasses and while the lens might have been fine the color of frames I had chosen were atrocious — for me; so dull that they looked dowdy, and certainly they did nothing for me. Another time, I purchased some house slippers while in a blue mood and they were of a most unpleasant style, not suitable at all.

This sort of thing happens very rarely these days, I am happy to relate, for I feel more equable than ever before in my life. Therefore, I am less likely to make a mistake in judgment.

Since I have been guided into the way of what I call 'Right Living', I have seen and learned many things which previously I had just taken for granted, thus missing many of the more real joys of life.

CHAPTER EIGHTEEN

MOVING one's home (as I believe I have mentioned before) is, to many people, a traumatic experience, and in our circumstances it definitely was no picnic for my household. Sometimes, in my idle moments, I would count up all the different homes where I had found myself at various times in my life. It was easily a good runner up with sheep-counting, if one had difficulty in inducing sleep and one had tried everything else. It was quite interesting to visit again, in my mind, some of the nice places and some not so nice, but each interesting in its own way; and I enjoyed recalling some of the associations I had made throughout my life.

There was the experience of quite young days, trying to ride a bicycle on a country road where I had to mount the machine on the grassy slope at the side of the road and, if possible, dismount the same way — unless I had fallen off in the meantime. 'Why all the fuss?' you may ask. Well I learned to ride on a man's bicycle since that was all there was available, and I never managed to get onto the thing in the accepted manner. However, I managed in the end to transport myself from one place to another, often 'losing my head' in an emergency and riding over small stones or anything else I might try to avoid. My sense of direction and balance would never win me a diploma, that was certain.

A certain charming gentleman of the district used to take a walk with his wife each evening and apparently he derived much interest and amusement in watching me while I engaged in the difficult maneuvers. However, I could forgive him for what I then considered his misplaced mirth, for this gentleman, who has now passed on, gave me a great deal of encouragement and guidance at a time when it was most needed and the association helped me to understand what life was all about; and for this I have always felt kindly towards this man — one of my earliest mentors.

FLIGHT OF THE PUSSYWILLOW

Although I did not realize it at the time, I see, on looking back, that I must have been something of a tomboy — and I was always falling and getting cuts and bruises. A few years later, after I had become a rather better bicycle operator, I decided I would like to try my luck on a motorcycle so I 'conned' a friend into letting me try. It was a nice sensation but I decided to stick to my 'cycle' as I had by then acquired a machine more in keeping with 'a lady' (with strings over the spokes of the rear wheel, which protected my clothing).

How these things stay in one's consciousness, having been indelibly impressed in the formative years. And there is another mini-story I must relate, for anything which can make us smile is worth recording — provided the amusement is not at the expense of another person's feelings: In my youth I was a regular churchgoer, sometimes twice on a Sunday but invariably once, as well as Sunday school in the afternoon. Often we had lay preachers taking the service because the Minister in charge of the diocese could not be in all the places at once. Some of our lay preachers had a most interesting message for the congregation, and I have always thought of one man in particular because he was such a good God-fearing person and, what was most important, he 'practiced what he preached' which was a simple and straightforward way of life. He was employed by a farmer in the capacity of 'shepherd', which occupation appealed to us children for wasn't he in the same occupation as that of his Master, his Leader, the entity whose concepts he followed? Yes, he was indeed a faithful disciple of the Good Shepherd, and for this he was respected. But it was not al- together for this reason that the memory of Old John has stayed with me; it was his natural manner — so friendly and genuine; and he spoke in just the same style whether he met one in the street or whether he was delivering a sermon. One Sunday morning, when he had been designated to take the service, everything went as usual and we were enjoying the hymns and the prayers — and then we came to the sermon.

Perhaps we had been a little late in starting the meeting, or the hymns might have taken longer than usual, or the prayers; after which we sat back to enjoy the discourse, ready to listen to John's theme for the day. He had been expounding his views for some minutes when suddenly he took out his watch from his vest pocket and announced, 'My goodness, it's late! I must not be too long for my Sarah Ann will have the dinner ready.' So the service finished quite promptly, with John the shepherd hurrying home to his Sarah

FLIGHT OF THE PUSSYWILLOW

Ann and no-one minding; instead, everybody loved him for his simple manner. This delightful old gentleman left his earthly shell many years ago but I will always retain a soft spot in my heart towards him. It seemed to please him that I had the same name as his wife, and when he saw me coming along the road towards him he would call out happily, 'Ah, here comes our Sarah Ann!'

And so, one pauses to contemplate, 'Where would we all be without our fond memories of past days?' They sure help to improve the present, and make a better TODAY.

So, there it was; soon we were making plans for the next important step in our lives, all the time wondering what this Tomorrow had in store for us. Cleo and Taddy were barely four months old, and they had been with us less than two of those months — barely time to get settled into the Family Routine. But even at that early age they were very alert, and once I very nearly suffered a heart attack where I couldn't find them anywhere in the apartment. Eventually, having searched in every other place, I had the stove pulled away from the wall in the kitchen and, with a sigh of relief, I saw those two miniature kittens emerging, looking surprised and slightly the worse for wear. They were such tiny creatures, even for kittens of their age, and that is why I called them 'miniature'.

It was fortunate that this time the proprietor of the store where we had bought our furniture was willing to take back everything. It was all in such good condition, and had been purchased so recently, that he had nothing to lose — deducting just enough to cover the cost of getting the goods back (although he had his own van), plus a little more to cover his 'overheads'; and he would still make a profit, he said. This arrangement was a great relief to us, and we were more than satisfied with the arrangement. Since we were going to be living in furnished accommodations again we had only our personal belongings to transfer, and as we had not had a preview of the place it was deemed wisest to take as little as possible, giving us more room to move around, as- suming there was that much space available.

For two nights before the journey it was necessary to stay in the Hotel at Fort Erie because we would be without furniture, linen, or anything, if we had stayed in the apartment.

The arrangement was awkward, but unavoidable, because the furniture was taken away two days before we left, while our personal things (suitcases, etcetera) would not be going until the evening before our trip to Prescott — our final destination. However, it all worked out satisfactorily; and in any case we couldn't have done much about it when the store proprietor was, in a way, doing us a favor, and we had to have the removal van on the only day it was available.

Difficult though it is to have to break up one's home, there are a few compensations — the most important being the wonderful feeling of 'freedom': Freedom from too many possessions, and freedom from getting into a rut. After all, there is still truth in the old saying, 'It's an ill wind that profits no-one.' So, indirectly, the press had propelled us out from a certain amount of security, and forward into an as yet unknown future with its unexplored experiences. The price had been costly; not only the loss of a loved creature, but financially; for even in our grief we have to live and sustain ourselves physically.

It entailed a certain amount of waiting, on each of those two days, before everything was cleared away from the apartment, so I was able to exercise my mental processes (which had become somewhat 'rusty' during the past months while we had been marking time). What a strange feeling to be sitting amongst a pile of suitcases and other packages, together with the furniture. And after the furniture had been taken, it was even more strange to be in an empty apartment with only one's personal goods. Have you ever noticed how an empty room 'echoes'? And how such weird impressions pervade the atmosphere?

I relived some of our experiences of the past year, and even further back — back to the time of the writing of 'The Third Eye' when we had been living in MOST DIFFICULT conditions. I often marveled how that book was ever written — the Guv typing while an irate neighbor banged on the adjoining wall because the typewriter was aggravating her nerves. In spite of all the obstacles, I could still recall a few pinpoints of shining light which were made possible by the Guv's patience and sense of humor; AND Miss Ku'ei with her own particular sparkle.

For some reason my thoughts kept dwelling on the kindness and tolerance of the Guv: How understanding he had been when my Silver Tabby had passed on; how he explained that, although the grief was mine, I was making it difficult for Mr. T. Cat to settle down in his new surroundings while I mourned for him. The Guv had taken me from the suburbs of London into

FLIGHT OF THE PUSSYWILLOW

the city to get a Cat magazine, where we could find an advertisement for Siamese kittens. He had not been feeling well, and I was not very interested in the venture, but eventually I began to see the sense of his suggestion and acted upon it. As usual the Guv knew best, and this resulted in the arrival of the Lady Ku'ei, who proved such a blessing to us — a definite one-person cat who careered around the curtains and furniture, and who (when I was alone with her) would let out a low growl, almost like a dog. We had been quite concerned, on the second day after her arrival, when we realized she had climbed a good way up the living room chimney. With the use of a mirror we could see her sitting there on a protruding ledge — refusing to be coaxed down and too far up the chimney for us to reach her. In the end the Guv had to drill a hole through the outside wall and make a space big enough for her to be reached and brought out. Quite amusing in retrospect but not so funny at the time.

I often envied the ability of the Guv and Miss Ku'ei to communicate so perfectly by telepathy; but I was fortunate in receiving any messages which were of special interest, and any which were meant for me. In those days of Miss Ku'ei's early life we had many creatures in our garden—baby shrews and mother shrews, and a delightful mole, with her young. It was a great pleasure to watch these people from our window.

One day a neighbor cat, or was it a 'stray' had wandered into the garden. Somehow it had got caught on the wire fencing dividing the gardens, and since it wore a collar it was unlikely that it was a stray. There it was — in a most undesirable situation; and if the Guv had not hurried out and rescued it, soon it would have been a dead cat — hanged by its own collar. And there was the starling who had been injured, and who was hidden amongst the foliage — almost ready for leaving this life. The Guv had stroked it . . . spoke to it . . . and helped it on its way to happier pastures. He explained to me that the bird could now depart knowing there was still LOVE and COMPASSION to be had amongst earth people — and thus the little creature would adjust all the more quickly to its next stage of existence.

I have often thought of the shelter that trees and other foliage have provided for nature creatures in their distress — for trees, especially, have far greater powers than is believed by the majority of people, not only physically but in the way of intelligence. Trees definitely are thinking entities, of a high order.

FLIGHT OF THE PUSSYWILLOW

As I dwelt upon memories of nature people, I remembered the time in South America when the Guv was standing by the window — looking out. When I inquired the reason for his sad expression, he remarked that he was just watching a bird who was coasting around trying to find a place to die.

By telepathy, the Guv knew that the bird's nest had been destroyed by vandals and the bird had lost the will to live. So, I thought, telepathy, too acute, can be a two-edged weapon.

Soon it would be time to leave the apartment, so I must not take too much more time with my reminiscences . . . but, before my eyes came the picture of a little rabbit which I had as a child. Somehow it found its way through a hole in an old sofa and disappeared into the interior, and my mother told me later that I wept the whole night through, wondering at the fate of my pet. But now time was passing; the suitcases and everything had been taken away to the station — so I would have to go too. Taking a last look around, locking the door, and leaving the keys with the Landlord nearby, I wandered over to check the luggage at the baggage department of the Canadian National Railroad Station, and then made my way to the Hotel to join the others. We were all tired and needed a good rest in preparation for the next day's journey. That night it was not necessary to count either sheep or houses — my relief was so great that we were finally ready, and sleep beckoned with open arms.

CHAPTER NINETEEN

THE Thousand Islands — a real wonderland; and that was the district we were bound for. I have often marveled that the name was not immortalized in some other manner than that of salad dressing. 'What kind of dressing would you like with the salad, ma'am?' is the frequently asked question on visiting a restaurant. If one is slow to answer the inquiry is followed by, The Thousand Islands, perhaps?'; and because it is so well known and palatable — which accounts for its popularity — that is what one takes in the end. Still, I think those beautiful and historical islands are worthy of being associated with something more inspiring than mere food.

You don't agree with me! Well, we are all entitled to our own opinion and I stick to mine.

It was a glorious day for traveling, and the flight did not take long, but we had to start out from Fort Erie by car for we took off from Welland, some miles away. There was no airport at Fort Erie, but the car ride was no problem. Miss Cleo and Miss Taddy did not like the noise of the plane; but now they are well-seasoned travelers, and that was the first of many trips by road, rail and air. The aforesaid remark brings to mind a radio program from England during the days of the second world war. The participants, it would be announced, had arrived by land, sea and air; and the name of the program was 'In Town Tonight', prepared by Peter Duncan — a very well-known radio personality. Sorry, another digression! So, back to the events of the day.

It was around three o'clock in the afternoon when we reached another non-commercial airport, near the city of Brockville, because Prescott being somewhat smaller did not have one, and from Brockville we had to drive the ten or twelve miles to our destination.

FLIGHT OF THE PUSSYWILLOW

Yes, the Cat People had completed their first flight . . . . and in the years to follow there would be more. I thought it fortunate that by reason of the day of their birth they ought eventually prove to become excellent travelers, especially air travelers, for is not the sign of Aquarius one of the three airy signs, and very futuristic?

Personally I enjoy flying, but the others of the family (human especially) are not so enamored with it. However, it was a case of Hobson's choice for there was no train between the two points, and a journey by road would have been too exhausting for all of us, taking about six hours, perhaps more. and the best route would have been through part of the U.S.A. which might have posed a few extra problems. So, after all, the air trip was worthwhile and we were able to provide a little pleasure for a Fort Erie friend who had done many services for us, and still continues to do so. This episode had its amusing side too, and it seems that if your mind is so tuned you can often see something funny in any situation. Since the aircraft had to return to Welland in any case, we thought Pauline might as well enjoy the trip, and she was most anxious to accompany us, but she had one small cause for concern: She had two young daughters and they were quite worried about the safety of their mother traveling homewards in the company of two men — the pilot and co-pilot. Of course Pauline considered it a huge joke, but it made her feel good to know that her children were so very concerned for her welfare.

With certain misgivings we approached the Daniels Hotel . . . and entered, inquiring for the manager, who soon appeared; so we introduced ourselves and soon we were directed to our suite, which proved to be eminently suitable.

Although we did not know it then, the year ahead was to prove one of the most satisfactory periods we had encountered for a long time. Ivan Miller did everything possible to make us comfortable, and our accommodation was quite adequate for our needs. Ivan took a great liking for our Cleo and Taddy, and he would greet them with, 'How are you Guys.' They had a great love for Ivan in return.

We seemed to have made a very satisfactory move, and I was reminded of a remark made some years previously, when we lived in Windsor, and we had a visitor from Upper Canada (from the Kingston area) who said, 'Why don't you come to live in the Kingston district, or further up the St. Lawrence river where all is calm and beautiful?' This person found Windsor too industrialized, and too low-lying. Well, I reflected, here we are, and soon we shall find out for ourselves whether we will like it or not. In the days to come we explored the area and came to know the surrounding district very well.

It was during those pleasant Prescott days that we came to know Mrs. Mary Ann Czermak from San Francisco, when she had reason to come to our part of the world; and I was speaking to her a few days ago when she mentioned that not only might I mention her in my story but that 'indeed she would be honored to receive mention'. So, thank you, Mary Ann! And I'm happy to know you still have pleasant memories of the Canadian food. Mrs. Czermak wanted to make something of her life besides just being a housewife, so the Guv suggested she study photography more deeply since she was an exceptionally good amateur photographer even then. Following his advice she now augments the family income by doing just that; and she specialized in photographing horses for a time, attending shows and meeting many interesting people. Since she was able to work in her own neighborhood, the greater part of the time, she was able to combine her lucrative hobby with her homemaking duties, which were not allowed to suffer at all. About seven months ago Mrs. Czermak acquired a little stray kitten (who is now a lovely cat), and just this morning I received a delightful picture of Cat Person Suzuki, sitting in a dignified pose inside a dishwashing bowl, if a pose in such a setting can be termed 'dignified'. I had mentioned in a recent letter that, judging from her handwriting, Mrs. Czermak had 'blossomed' since the advent of Suzuki; her writing was more rounded and pleasant. She agreed with my comments, saying she felt herself to be a different person, and continued: 'Nobody has ever shown me such unconditional love as this little Girl Cat.' And it seems the whole family agrees that it's impossible to imagine the household without her. A nice tribute! Mrs. Czermak has quite a liking for Canada and its beautiful scenery, having visited this country several times. She came to New Brunswick while we were there and later paid us a visit in Montreal. She took a trip by sea from Saint John, New Brunswick, to Digby, Nova Scotia, on the ferry, and she was so enthralled that she ran out of film before the outing ended.

She amused me the other day when she mentioned the most delightful Bay of Fundy prawns she had enjoyed at the Moon Palace Restaurant in Saint John, where we had dined one evening. 'What a memory', I told her . . . 'To remember after all these years'. 'Yes', she said, 'I can still see in my mind's eye the lovely reddish color of those prawns.'

It appears to me at this moment that a good title for this book might be 'Flowers of Friendship', for so many pleasant incidents come to mind which cannot be ignored. I have mentioned previously that friendships do not come easily, and neither do they — quality definitely being preferable to quantity. It just occurred to me the other day that my few personal friends are owned by Cat People, and that makes the association all the more precious. Another truth has dawned upon me, and it is this: You can have a really close association, leading to a firm and lasting friendship, with someone you have never met physically. I have such a friend in Tessamarie — and her Siamese cat, Keeta. In our more difficult times we have been able to provide encouragement and pleasure for each other, through letters and very infrequent telephone conversations. This is a person for whom I have much admiration, and the only problem I encounter is in trying to decipher her minute handwriting; but this is quickly overcome by using a small magnifier, and her cheerful comments are well worth the effort. At my bedside I have a little book of Oriental Wisdom which Tessamarie kindly presented to me, and I enjoy reading the philosophy of Confucius, Lao-Tse and others.

Having mentioned a number of feminine acquaintances and friends, and lest it be thought one may have an aversion to masculine companionship, let me hasten to record that such is not the case . . . my few close associates do include the opposite sex.

Not everyone who reads this wants to hear about ALL the people who interest me, or who are interested in me, but I might mention two or three of the persons I have known for a few years. The first two have the same name but they are spelt in different ways — there is John (who I have known the longest), and Jon (who came into our life a little later). Both these gentlemen are friends of my Family and we have come to know each other quite well. John has visited us a number of times and we have spent many interesting moments in each other's company. A follower of the Guv s beliefs, and an avid reader of the Rampa books, he has introduced me to a few other interesting authors. One of the nicest things John ever did was to bring along the story of Jonathan Livingston Seagull by Richard Bach, because otherwise I might have missed that delightful story.

The other friend, Jon, is another person who finds great benefit in following the teachings of Lobsang Rampa, and he has often commented how his life has changed for the better since he has known the Guv. Jon is interested in photography and he has made astonishing progress in a matter of two years and, since he is owned by two beautiful cats, he is never short of a photographic subject; and some of his pictorial scenes are something to be remembered. Living in British Columbia gives one many opportunities for making artistic reproductions of mountain, ocean, and city life. This friend paid us a visit last month and just before he arrived I had cut my finger. 'Look,' I said, 'I have sliced the end off my finger.' He looked (although the sight of blood makes him feel squeamish), considered for a moment; then, with a whimsical smile commented, 'My goodness, but don't you think that is a drastic method of trying to lose weight?' We enjoy his sense of humor even though at times it might seem rather misplaced.

Another gentleman of our acquaintance lives in England and he visited us here in Canada some years ago, so it was my pleasant duty to show him around a corner of our country. The particular Province was that of Quebec and the city was Montreal, so there was quite a lot to see in that particular corner; and, being an ardent horticulturist, he was particularly interested in the Botanical Gardens, where we took quite a large number of photographs of the trees and plants and various flowers.

We dined together two or three times in one or another of Montreal's delightful restaurants, and the topics of conversation were interesting and enjoyable to both of us and are still remembered with pleasure. One has to be prepared for all sorts of remarks in the course of one's life, and Mr. Sowter startled me somewhat as I was casually contemplating my amethyst ring which had been a gift, the amethyst being a stone which I understood induced calmness and placidity in the wearer, and I believe it had such an effect. Whether it was said in fun or seriously I did not know but, after contemplating me for a few moments, Mr. Sowter suddenly remarked, 'Mrs. Rampa, I would have thought you had progressed beyond the wearing of jewelry.' I must say that his comment gave me food for thought, but then I decided there is nothing wrong with wearing jewelry; if so, it would be strange that so many church leaders, such as Bishops, wear an amethyst. Well, if Mr. Sowter should read these pages I am telling him that I no longer own that ring — not because I did not like it or believe in it, but for a reason which is not relevant to my story.

Well Mr. Sowter thoroughly enjoyed his visit to Canada, and amongst the items he found to take back with him was a beautiful Rosenthal bust of

FLIGHT OF THE PUSSYWILLOW

Nefertiti, something else to remind him of a pleasant experience, and he says he has placed her in an ideal position at the top of the stairway in his home, where he is able to greet her in passing.

Mr. Sowter is a dedicated bird lover and I admire him for the interest he takes in the R.S.P.B. (the Royal Society for the Protection of Birds). As gifts, he presents to his friends such items as Bird Calendars, table covers with bird designs, and the like. The other day I received a delightful handkerchief, and printed on it was a design of beautiful feathers in various colors and shades of colors. Truly a gentleman of excellent taste and sensitivity — for all this is done in the interest of the Bird Society of Great Britain.

CHAPTER TWENTY

IT was our intention to stay at the Daniels Hotel for a short period only, simply to give us sufficient time to look around and find a furnished house or some other dwelling more permanent and home-like than we could expect from hotel living. This was easier said than done for property was not so simple to obtain, either for rent or even to buy — the latter not of interest to us in any case. There is much activity in the district, factories such as R.C.A. and the large Dupont Company; therefore, all the workers had to be housed and this was a direct cause of overcrowding in that little town.

Strangely enough, Prescott sported only one hotel, although previously there had been several; all of them gradually dis- appearing; some probably having become too decrepit for further occupation while one, at least, had been destroyed by fire just a few months earlier.

After a week or two of vain searching we approached Ivan, the hotel manager, with the intention of asking about a longer stay in the suite we occupied. 'Your hotel is very nice' we informed him, 'so perhaps we can come to terms with you regarding a longer tenancy, if you are agreeable.'

Ivan's response was indicative of his whole attitude throughout our stay and we quickly came to an arrangement. He was pleased to hear we were finding the place so satisfactory, and we sighed with relief knowing we might enjoy the remainder of the summer months without the dreary grind of home-hunting.

One of the worst experiences we encountered was the invasion of those little creatures, shad flies. They came all around the window screens, and in one's hair; even on the food if one did not take extra care. When these creatures first appeared we wondered whatever was happening; but the whole cycle was completed in a matter of about two weeks — to our immense satisfaction. This invasion seems to prevail in just a few areas, and they seemed to be particularly attracted to Prescott. It was our first, and only, encounter with shad flies for which we were truly thankful.

The weeks passed, and occasionally one or two members of the Family would go off to Brockville where there was a greater variety of opportunities for shopping. The drive along by the river was a delight, and often we wished we could find a place to live somewhere along that stretch of ten or twelve miles.

It was in Brockville that we met the veterinarian who would be caring for Miss Cleo and Miss Taddy, and we came to know this gentleman quite well for all cats need a check-up periodically, just as human animals do. By the time those little people were just a few months old we realized they were not very strong physically, and when Taddy developed a limp we were quite concerned. Gradually the time approached when we had to prepare for the operation which is required for all little girl cats if they are going to be raised as 'pets' only. That is the spaying operation which is per- formed so that there will be no likelihood of them producing baby cats.

We had noticed when we took them out for a drive that they had some difficulty in maintaining their balance, and we were somewhat concerned about this also. Dr. Wang, who had given the whole situation a good deal of thought, decided to have some X-rays taken prior to the operation. He was rather puzzled about Taddy's limp, and he pointed out that there was a danger she might injure herself while struggling under the anesthetic so we would be wiser to find out the cause first. It was not a simple procedure to place two cats in position to have their limbs X-rayed, but being nice helpful girl cats, the pictures were obtained and interpreted to show there really was cause for concern: It was found that these two little people had what is known as osteoporosis — a softening of their bones; and there was evidence of a number of minor fractures in each case.

It was necessary to provide them with plenty of calcium tablets, supplemented with Pablum (baby food), which they enjoyed when mixed with the concentrated juice from a little cooked lean beef (they will not take fatty juice! If it is 'fatty', one has to cool it in the refrigerator and then remove the solid fat before heating and offering it to the creatures). If possible, it is better that they should take the preparation themselves, but in this case I spoon-fed them so they were sure of getting it, and each would have her share.

FLIGHT OF THE PUSSYWILLOW

We were not in a position to play about — it was too serious; and a few months later we had the satisfaction of seeing Cleo and Taddy becoming more healthy, Taddy having lost her limp, and even though it was well past the usual time for spaying, at last they had the operation . . . and soon they were home again.

I have to comment here that life in hotels is not the ideal situation for two Siamese queens during their 'calling' periods. However, Dr. Wang kindly supplied some little pills, to be used during those times, and this made life more tolerable for the Family, the other guests, and especially for the little people themselves.

We have kept in touch with this particular veterinarian during the ensuing years, and we just heard from him last week. I have been asked whether he is of Chinese nationality, and though I would not mind whether he were Chinese or any other nationality, I have to say he is of Norwegian descent, and I will always have a feeling of gratitude towards him for detecting the deficiency with which our Cat People were beset and which delayed for a time their natural growth.

During that summer after our arrival in Prescott, the Guv was able to write one of his books. He must have felt the atmosphere to be conducive to writing in order to achieve this in the rather limited space, especially since it was such an excellent piece of work — probably my favorite Lobsang Rampa volume, apart from 'Living with the Lama' and 'You, Forever', which of course is a 'study' book. Yes, I found quite a lot of humor in 'Chapters of Life' and, indeed, the dedication was in favor of Miss Cleopatra Rampa and Miss Tadalinka Rampa, who, if the Guv had not been more alert than they, might have chewed up the pages as soon as they were completed. In those days, due to their deficiency, they would chew anything they could get their claws on (twine, rubber bands, etc.), and it meant a constant vigil to keep all these things out of their way. I was warned that rubber bands could easily cause an obstruction of the bowel, while Taddy seemed to root them out from nowhere.

However, it was all well worth the effort of caring for them. for now I have two beautiful cat companions who are loyal, loving, and definitely a credit to the Family. Mentioning Dr. Peter Wang, the Norwegian, brings to my mind a book about Norway, written by a popular author of my young days. The book described Norway beautifully — the fjords, the beautiful scenery; and the author was Marie Corelli. O, yes, the title of the work was 'Thelma', a name which I like very much, and I am reminded of it each time I meet Miss Thelma Dumont who has done so much in the way of helping me with this book, such as typing, pointing out errors for correction, and showing a real interest in the project. While copying from my rough typescript, she has made a point of commenting upon any parts which she found of special interest; and, judging from her remarks, I know she has been reading it in detail. One day, in the early pages, Thelma suddenly asked: 'Are Ku'ei and Fifi still with you?' And when I had to answer, 'No, I'm afraid not,' she looked quite sad. 'I rather wish you hadn't told me,' she said. She is a very sensitive and capable person and without her help and real interest it is doubtful my story would have reached even this stage. Her sadness disappeared when I was able to tell her, in answer to her query whether the Guv was still around, that, 'Yes, he is,' and she exclaimed genuinely, 'I'm so glad.'

So the days and weeks rolled by and soon everyone was preparing for Expo '67, the big Centennial celebration which was to be held in Montreal. Gradually it came to our notice that various persons were planning to visit Expo '67 and at the same time intended to 'stop off' at Prescott to pay their respects to Lobsang Rampa. It seemed a wonderful idea except that we did not welcome visitors at any time unless they were invited, which was a rare occurrence. Since Montreal was a mere two hours drive away from us we became more than a little concerned, for we knew it would be no problem for anyone to find us since Prescott was not a big place.

Ivan was very busy, in anticipation of welcoming Centennial visitors, and the girls in his coffee shop were being fitted out with their last-century dresses, while Ivan himself started to grow a beard. The scene was changing and we were in rather a quandary once more. It seemed that, for 'the duration', we really would have to find some place to stay which was a little less prominent; but — where? Soon it would be one year since we had arrived at the Daniels, and since it was impossible to secure anything more private we began to look further afield.

One day I happened to mention that New Brunswick seemed to be a nice area, perhaps it was worth considering.

'I have heard that the scenery is rather like the Irish countryside,' I commented. So the idea gradually formed in our minds and before very long we were making inquiries and preparations for the trek from Ontario, across the Province of Quebec, into New Brunswick. We had decided upon the city of Saint John as being most suitable because it was situated by the ocean, which we decided would be a nice change after the St. Lawrence river area of Upper Canada.

Ivan seemed sad that we were leaving and he smiled when we suggested he would need our suite to accommodate all the important visitors who would be arriving during the summer.

At last the Day arrived, a lovely May day, when we de- parted in a fairly roomy; if not too modern, aircraft; and the journey took somewhere around three hours. It was late afternoon when we reached Saint John, Atlantic time being one hour ahead of Prescott's 'Eastern daylight'.

It was a lovely time of the year to be living in New Brunswick and we found the people quite friendly though a little aloof until one had lived there long enough to 'prove' one's self. The apartment which we rented overlooked the Harbor, and from the uppermost floor (which was the thirteenth) we could watch ships entering and leaving the Port of Saint John. The superintendent of the building was very interested in his job and he looked after the tenants extremely well. He was especially helpful towards the older people, and his patience seemed inexhaustible.

This was another quiet time in our lives and we made the most of it, enjoying a drive around the district occasionally; and the Cat Persons were very satisfied to go on these leisurely trips.

As winter approached we liked the milder temperature since Prescott could be extremely cold, with more than a fair share of snow. Of course snow soon melts in coastal towns and cities, but it seems that Saint John has suffered some quite dreadful snowstorms during the past winter. Certainly the fates were kind to us that winter; but, in passing. I might add that anyone who plans to pay a visit to that part of the Maritimes might be well-advised to include an umbrella in their luggage.

CHAPTER TWENTY-ONE

IT is election day here in Alberta, and the first week of Spring — by the calendar anyway. In reality we have snow and cold winds from the north sweeping along at twenty miles per hour; and when I awoke this morning the temperature was six degrees (F.) above zero, and the weather man kindly informed us that equaled 1° C. Last month it was much warmer and everybody was preparing to cast off their winter clothing, but now it is back to big winter boots and scarves to keep us warm from head to toe. Still we expect the warm Chinook air will be along soon so that we can all smile again. Someone may say, 'But what is all this to do with your story?'; and I have to answer, 'Well, it IS my story — moving around the country with my Family, feeling the atmosphere of the various provinces, and comparing them.'

As I start to write this, the last part of my book, my mind wanders back to the Maritimes, to Saint John in particular. Although the Guv was even then using a wheel chair for moving around, he was still not too incapacitated. We enjoyed idling around the road outside the apartment building, the Guv with his wheel chair, accompanied either by Buttercup or me; and soon the local residents came to know us, often stopping for a chat. One day when Buttercup was accompanying the Guv she was approached by a small girl who had been hanging around and viewing them with interest. At last, having summoned sufficient courage, she went right up and addressed Buttercup. 'Do you take him out every day, Miss?', she said. Then she dashed off, without waiting for an answer, her courage suddenly deserting her, leaving the Guv and Buttercup highly amused.

This episode reminds me of something which happened just a few days ago when a young man came here on an errand. Being the son of one of our friends he had heard about Dr. Rampa and he was most eager to see the Guv, having combed his hair specially we were told. The Guv was not at all

FLIGHT OF THE PUSSYWILLOW

well that evening but he could not bear to disappoint a young man who had made a point of tidying himself up for the occasion. It was a pleasurable event lasting all of fifteen minutes, and Andrew was off home again. Later when we talked to our friend, Andrew's father, to inquire whether the young man had found the visit worthwhile, we were told, 'He said he was sorry for the old fellow as he has no legs below the knees'. For a moment we were nonplussed and then we realized the Guv had been sitting in the lotus position, which he finds most comfortable, and over the sheets it looked exactly like an amputation. Another cause for amusement, all of which helps to keep us cheerful.

Yes, it was a happy time in Saint John; and the Guv wrote another book, the idea for the cover being taken from a photograph of that time, where he was holding a prayer-wheel and a begging bowl. For those who may be interested, the title of the book was 'Beyond the Tenth'.

Our home was not very far from the Bay of Fundy and the Reversing Falls, so named because at a certain point under the bridge a stretch of water on the Saint John river collides with water from the Falls, causing a reversal of the tide; and this is a very popular tourist attraction. The tides are higher than anywhere else in the world, running into the inlet between Nova Scotia and New Brunswick and rising up to 60 feet.

Some people say that distance and the passing of time lend a sort of enchantment, and that things were never so good at the time they happened as they are in retrospect; but of our stay in the Maritimes, I can only say that we enjoyed and appreciated it at the time.

Water is possessed of a magnetic quality and the sea has an added mysticism. Many are the tales told by some of the Atlantic fishermen and older residents of strange happenings at sea and in the remote districts, tales the validity of which we could well appreciate.

The New Brunswickers are a proud group of loyalists and their province provides much of Canada's history. There is a small island a short distance from the harbor which is the burial place of many Irishmen who came to Canada in the days of the great potato famine, but who developed a plague and never reached the mainland of the New World.

They had not been allowed to leave their ship, by the authorities, for fear they should spread the disease which had been caused by starvation and overcrowding. Therefore, as they died they found their last resting place on

99

that little piece of land.

Off the mainland there is another place of interest, Grand Manan island, where President Roosevelt kept a summer home and where he spent many vacations, away from the problems of his high office.

After a stay of about a year and a half, it was necessary to make another break in our life-pattern and so we went to Montreal; but the following year we were drawn back to New Brunswick for what proved to be a rather short and somewhat distressing period.

On our second visit we stayed in the Admiral Beatty Hotel for a few weeks while we waited for our apartment which was not yet ready. The hotel manager was most helpful and treated us extremely well, as did his dining room supervisor who also acted in the capacity of hostess and who was always most solicitous for our welfare.

Everybody was helpful in Saint John, especially the two men who operated a fish truck, and who transported the Guv (together with his wheel chair) when he had to move from the railway station to the hotel and later from the hotel to the apartment. These men manipulated that hoist in a most professional manner — and they were obviously delighted to be of service.

While we stayed at the Admiral Beatty, Prince Philip, Duke of Edinburgh, happened to visit the city, and when he passed through the foyer we had the pleasure of seeing His Royal Highness. Everyone seemed excited when they heard him coming down the stairway (the elevators, it seemed, were not swift enough for him), and as he strode past the crowd they waved enthusiastically and applauded him. We seem to have had more glimpses of the Royal Family in Canada than we ever did in England for the Queen Mother visited Saint John on our earlier stay, and since the Royal Yacht 'Britannia' had docked in the harbor we were able to look out and see Her Majesty as she made frequent trips to and from her temporary home. And of course we had the opportunity of seeing Queen Elizabeth the Second herself a few years earlier.

When we lived in Montevideo, President Goulart of Brazil came on a visit — and there was a reception right below our apartment building, so we were able to stand out on the balcony and watch the proceedings, at the same time getting some photographs of the occasion, and it was most interesting and quite exciting.

FLIGHT OF THE PUSSYWILLOW

Another interesting and rather exciting incident occurred around that period when the then ex-President Peron tried to stage a come-back from his exile in Spain. The plane carrying Juan Peron and his party passed right over our building on its way to Brazil where negotiations took place regarding entry into Argentina. Unfortunately for him, the ex-President was not allowed to return to his country; but he persevered and eventually regained his position as President, though only briefly. Thus it is with rulers, heads of State; often their positions are so uncertain that today's prince can very easily become the beggar of tomorrow. Yes, a borrowed phrase!

I hope that little backward look into yesterday is not considered too much of a digression; and now we return to the pleasant life of Saint John, which was all too short-lived. Miss Cleo and Miss Taddy liked the hotel because there was so much action; different people to see and many things of interest happening. Two or three times each week we used to sit in the hotel lobby, just so that these little people could have their recreation; and sometimes a guest would come up to see them and chat with us for a while. Everybody admired our Cat People and I enjoyed having an excuse to chat, especially if the person had something of interest to impart. Once we met two nice young girls from Quebec city, and they extolled the wonders of their city with much gusto; and I wished I could have seen this place for myself because many people have expressed delight over its beauty. Another time a young man came over to us, remarking that he was a representative for a company of Pet supplies, actually Hartz Mountain (whose cat litter we had always used), and he expressed interest in the traveling basket we were using.

I mentioned a company which I had known in England, a supplier of medicine for pets — various cat powders and the like. It was a well known company, and the young man was interested to hear that my Silver Tabby's photograph had looked out on the world from various drugstores and food shops throughout the country after the company had obtained the original picture from us, during the years of the Second World War. It had seemed strange (after T. Catt had gone to his heavenly home) to walk into a store and see his likeness still gazing placidly around and often I felt sad at the thought that he was no longer with us in the flesh.

Apart from visitors, many local people came into the hotel, some passing through the lobby and into the jewelry store of Henry Birks, the store and the people being a source of constant interest. This time was not wasted because it prevented Cleo and Taddy from getting too nervous as they had been for a while in Prescott before we started to take them downstairs to the lobby at the Daniels Hotel.

Eventually the apartment was ready for us, in the same building where we had lived previously, there being very few high-rise buildings in the district — especially with a view of the sea, although in the intervening years I believe this has been remedied somewhat and there is more choice of accommodation. Apartment living was something new to the people and they did not take well to the idea; but later the whole complex was occupied and soon there was a waiting list. It was an eminently suitable life-style for anyone waiting to purchase a house, or being temporarily transferred in their job, and one came across a number of newly married people full of the excitement of starting a home, discussing the price of wall-to-wall carpeting, etc., while waiting for the mailman in the lobby (which was a general meeting place each morning.)

It never seems to pay to become too complacent for immediately we sit back, relax, and think we will 'take it easy' we are jerked back to alertness and action. Barely two months after getting settled into the new home, sadness entered our lives once again: The Guv suddenly suffered acute pain and he was so sick that we had to get medical help. This led to a stay in a Saint John Hospital and we all felt very sad at being parted from each other. Miss Cleo and Miss Taddy were very unhappy, even though they could communicate quite easily; but it was not the same as having the Guv at home where they could be close beside him.

It just happened that, during the stay in hospital, there was a 'flu epidemic' in the district; so — no visitors. Really, the Guv must have felt very isolated, as did we all, and we were happy when the day came that he was able to return home. Cleo and Taddy were quite excited, yet rather shy, not having seen the Guv for the best part of a week. It was during this stay in hospital that the Guv was told he could expect to live for only a few months and he should keep a suitcase packed in anticipation of an early return to the hospital. 'You'll be back,' he was told in a matter of fact tone by one of the doctors. Unfortunately that was the unhappiest experience — the apparent lack of feeling towards a patient, and we can only tell ourselves that perhaps the doctor was sick himself or perhaps he had forgotten the hypocritical oath of his profession.

FLIGHT OF THE PUSSYWILLOW

It was another milestone in our lives — a turning point; and one only hoped the medical profession might be proved wrong. At the same time we felt we must not blind ourselves to the fact that nothing is certain and we should be prepared, in case those professional men should be proved correct in their prognosis. On the other hand, any one of us can be mistaken, whether we be medical or lay persons, and I, have here before me a quotation by Maimonides, Greek philosopher, which seems very appropriate so I will pass it on:

'May there never develop in me the notion that my education is complete but give me the strength and leisure and zeal continually to enlarge my knowledge.'

A concept worth following, and I found these words on the cover of some medical educational material.

In this case the medicos were proved wrong, but nevertheless it was a time of great concern, and I suppose we were worried underneath — if not consciously.

In the following few months the family was drawn closer together as we sat and chatted, or just sat, thinking each our own thoughts. On several evenings each week we used to view cine films which we had rented from the National Film Library, and some of them were quite educational, others amusing. Watching Buster Keaton making a train journey across Canada was quite hilarious and we all enjoyed the cartoons. The curator of the Museum, who had been our neighbor, kindly lent us some more films and these were greatly appreciated. We saw beautiful scenes, many from Europe, and especially good was one taken in Germany where the scenery and buildings held us enthralled. Then there was a short silhouette type film which we refer to even now because it gave us so much pleasure, its title being, 'The Grasshopper and The Ant'; Mr. Grasshopper being a delightful character who loved and lived Today — never caring for Tomorrow and its problems. Miss Ant was a severe lady who chastised Mr. Grasshopper for not preparing for Winter, but he still did not bother; while in the end Miss Ant mellowed, and the film ended with everyone happy and friendly; and it was one of the nicest little nature pictures I ever saw, written and produced by a German lady.

It was a hard, uphill fight for the Guv and to us, the on- lookers. Nothing short of a miracle how he kept going with all the pain he suffered; but even so, he sat down and wrote another book — telling of his most recent experiences. As I look back I have come to realize that he himself could not have been sure how long he would be able to continue living.

The most unpleasant aspect was the lack of cooperation from the treatment point of view, and I was puzzled as to why no one had talked to me regarding the illness. Even when I went to deliver a few personal things to the Guv during his stay there in the hospital I was greeted in a quite uncivil manner. I had not wanted to visit the ward knowing visitors were not allowed at that time, but the attitude seemed to be that I was trying to 'gate crash' my way in.

So, it was due to the lack of medical interest and care that we would leave New Brunswick for the second time. The Guv has himself written about all this so there is no need for me to enlarge upon it.

We were going to miss the calm, placid life of the Maritimes; and of course we would miss that delicacy which is peculiar to Nova Scotia and New Brunswick, the fiddlehead.

CHAPTER TWENTY-TWO

So it was back to Montreal, and Habitat, for the second time; but the circumstances would be in many ways a great deal more satisfactory than on our first visit, for we were, in a way, returning to friends. The administrator of Habitat had kept in touch with us and he was to have everything ready for our comfort while we would be located temporarily in one of the guest apartments.

On the morning of our departure, Saint John was shrouded in fog, so we ran into our first problem — no planes leaving the airport. When we received a telephone call at breakfast time to tell us we would have to travel to Fredericton by road, we did not feel too happy. Still there was nothing we could do about it, but we were concerned as to how the Guv would manage the journey which was being made longer because of the weather.

Eventually we started out, and we had to have two cars for our family of three adults, two Cat Persons, and our luggage. Miss Cleo and Miss Taddy went with me in the first car because the Guv preferred to travel behind so he could more easily keep his mind, and his eyes, on us; and periodically I would look around to wave, showing him we were doing all right. We had said our goodbyes to the superintendent who told us he was very sorry to lose such nice tenants and good friends, and he said he would keep in touch with us while perhaps one day we might return. I wondered how the Cat People would behave on what, for them, was a fairly lengthy car ride; but any worries I might have had proved groundless for they were extremely quiet and ladylike during the sixty mile drive. I had a suspicion that the Guv must have had a word with them, and of course they knew he was keeping an eagle eye in their direction.

As we drove along my thoughts wandered, as usual, and I have always found that the soothing purr of the engine is most conducive to day-dreaming — providing one is not driving I suppose. Many people seem to experience a certain amount of disassociation while at the wheel of a car, though enjoying the relaxation, and often finding the solution to a problem.

As I thought of our situation and the Guv's deterioration in health, I realized the fact that the years were passing and we were getting older, and not one of us expects to live forever. I thought of how (especially in the North American continent) everyone wants to remain young, going to all lengths in clothes and beauty aids to maintain the illusion.

No one would disagree that it is nice to remain young, and not many of us look forward with joy to advancing years; and most of us pass through a phase of mild 'panic' at the idea of becoming old, or even elderly.

Having passed through most of Shakespeare's seven stages, I feel it is in order to make a few comments — the most important being that getting old is a most interesting experience, and a time when most things cease to be a cause for worry. You have more time to enjoy what is around you for you cannot easily go rushing around, especially if you are 'out of breath' with little or no physical effort.

At various times in my life I have been reminded about 'age' and its importance. For many months after I was born I was always 'Baby', and perhaps I earned the title for I was just beginning to walk at eighteen months. At seven years I knew and envied a girl of eleven, believing her to be quite adult; and, along with my friends of that period, decided that were we not married by the age of twenty-one we might as well give up! By the time the magic twenty-one was reached it was neither the time for getting married or for giving up; and anyhow, in my mind seventeen had been the age of magic. Just about that time I had the misfortune to be hospitalized, and doctors seemed to be buzzing all around. 'Your name?' they inquired; and when I told them they looked glum and uninterested. 'Your age?' came next.

'Ah, that is more interesting' they answered when I told them 'Twenty-one'.

It must have been about twenty years later that someone drew attention to my age again. I was in conversation when the other person suddenly remarked: 'You must have been quite attractive when you were younger.' Not a very well- mannered person, I concluded. When, a few years later, I was making a transatlantic crossing by plane, in the company of a young girl, one of the passengers inquired whether she was my granddaughter. Now, I felt, I was really arriving — but I was to have yet another reminder: A year or two ago, I was in a bank one day buying a money order when I was asked: 'Are you a senior citizen?' In answer to my surprised expression and inquiry, 'Why?', I received the answer, 'Senior citizens do not have to pay any charges for money orders: Ah well, a few more years, I suppose, and someone will come along to help me across the street or something, with the comment, 'I expect you have been around for a long time, Lady!' And then I will know I have really ARRIVED.

So we reached Fredericton and eventually Montreal airport after a tiring flight, and the Guv absolutely exhausted, with fewer facilities for the deplaning of disabled persons than had existed at Fredericton. Another drive, a few miles along the Expressway, and we turned in towards Habitat where I noticed a few signs which had been absent when we left. Many people used to get lost trying to find their way around, but now it seemed the situation had been remedied.

After winding our way around the grounds at last we reached the entrance where we were welcomed by the senior commissionaire who we had known before, and who had been there since the days of Expo '67. On reaching the guest apartment we found Mr. Gobeille was waiting for us, in a fierce June heatwave, and no air conditioning since the electricians were in the midst of one of their frequent strikes. Mr. Gobeille appeared very pleased at our return and we enjoyed a few minutes chat together.

Cité du Havre, the site of Habitat, is almost an island and quite an interesting place to live, especially for those who like water and being near ships. We used to gaze out of the window and see craft from all over the world, so near that one could reach out and almost touch them. In summer it was pleasant as the temperature was ten degrees lower than the city of Montreal, but by the same token the ten degrees made quite a difference in the winter months when one almost got one's nose frozen off if one ventured outside.

There was very little choice of apartments so we had to settle for one which had a delightful view over the harbor but which had its entrance below ground level, which meant descending about fifteen stairs. Most of the apartments, or suites, were situated on two floors, and the bedrooms were either upstairs or, just as frequently, downstairs. Definitely a new way of living, but apparently quite popular for soon there was a waiting list. And the type of tenant was very mixed, consisting of doctors, musicians, writers and artists; also teachers; and various nationalities, all of whom seemed to get along well together. Since the Cité du Havre was with- out public transport we had our own private bus operating as far as the city, taking tenants to within a short distance of their places of work and delivering their children to school. without this service Habitat would not have been so popular because it was in a way quite isolated; no postal facilities for instance, and only one small food store where it was possible to obtain staple foods such as milk, bread, eggs and a few fruits and vegetables, with the usual canned foods and dry goods.

The man who operated the store was a unique character and many were the stories he told about the activities at Habitat in the days of Expo '67. Unfortunately his lease expired and he left for another position so he was greatly missed by the tenants. It was a marvel to us how Mr. P. always had fresh bread on hand, even when there could not possibly have been a baker's delivery. We later realized that Mr. P's version of fresh bread was bread which had been refrigerated. Still it is colorful personalities such as he which give an added zest to life, and it was an acknowledged fact that Mr. P. always seemed to achieve what anyone else would have deemed impossible.

I took a number of photographs around that time because it was possible to get some delightful pictures of the ships and the water from the walk-way on the tenth floor. And again we rented films from the Film Library; but it was not so interesting as the first time in Saint John — perhaps we had seen all the best ones, or we were getting too used to them.

There was one incident which amused us when our friend Jon came to visit us, and he joined us in viewing a medical film which was somewhat gory. If you remember, Jon cannot stand the sight of a bleeding finger, or anything like that, and this film happened to be taken in the operating theatre while an operation was in progress. Jon began to look pale and the Guv suggested he should have a stimulant before he passed out, having already left the room once. I took the phial and, wrapping it in a tissue, broke it and pushed it towards his face with the admonition, 'Here, sniff this.' So he took one breath and nearly fell over, gasping, 'Are you trying to finish me off?'

I must agree that sometimes the sight of blood makes me feel a little queasy myself, and I was a bit worried one Saturday when I was preparing lunch — I cut my finger and we couldn't stop the flow. The Guv fixed it temporarily and suggested I take myself off to the hospital; so I went quickly, via the Habitat limousine which just happened to be available. Buttercup accompanied me to the emergency department where we waited a few minutes; and then, after all details had been supplied, my finger received attention. I was given a bowl of warm water and told to 'stick it in there and clean it up'. Cleo and Taddy were very concerned, and when we returned home they looked a bit surprised to see us so soon while the Guv had done his best to reassure them, in spite of Taddy's telepathic inquiry, 'Do you think we will ever see Ma again.'

These two little people seemed to like Habitat, partly because there was plenty of room to play and have fun — running up and down stairs and hiding in various corners.

We used to drive over the bridge to St. Lambert where our French Canadian veterinarian had his office, and he treated Cleo and Taddy very well. He is a most conscientious person, and it was through Dr. Wang that we found him.

We were introduced to another Canadian way of life, that of the 'Drive-In' Restaurant. A friend suggested it was time the Cat People furthered their education, so we went once more to the St. Lambert district and enjoyed a hamburger and coffee while Cleo and Taddy were fascinated with the other patrons who were parked quite near us.

St. Lambert revives a sad memory too, in that the Quebec cabinet minister Pierre La Porte was held captive in a house not far away — and it was a distressing time while the F.L.Q. members were so active. Everyone in Quebec and all of Canada, and indeed the whole world, was shocked when they learned of M. La Porte's fate. And we had the unhappy experience of witnessing the cavalcade of F.L.Q. members, their car loaded with dynamite and accompanied by police as they passed by our window on the way to Expo grounds to hand over another captive — the British Trade Minister, Mr. Jasper Cross. Those were frightening days when many people dared not leave their homes in the evenings for fear they might be kidnapped; and Montreal's night life suffered greatly.

During the summer and fall we spent a lot of time sitting on the bank of the Habitat grounds watching the ships of various countries arriving and departing; and we could hear music across the water from 'Man and His World', the annual fair which followed Expo. And we would walk among the plants and flowers in the more cultivated areas, the Guv using his wheel chair, stopping to point out something of particular interest.

One day, when I was feeling less than cheerful and some- what sorry for myself, we went out and he showed me a little red flower, suggesting I might study it — meditate upon it, instead of dwelling upon my own problems. At the same time he suggested I might take to heart the following words:

'Let me think of others that I may forget myself.' Just a few words with a big meaning! So I made up a 'card' and tried to live up to its message.

From the medical aspect it was more reassuring because the doctor we had was very much of a humanitarian and he never minded making a visit at any time during the day or night. His wife, Joan, who I mention by name because she suggested I should, had written to us previously, having en-joyed the Lobsang Rampa books, and this was the start of an association which has lasted up to the present time.

Our nearest neighbor was a member of the medical profession and we enjoyed chatting with him on the all too rare occasions that we found time to meet. After we had left Habitat, his wife (another Joan) adopted our friends, the sparrows, who had come to our patio every morning for their breakfast. One day, when we were talking together by telephone she told me that when she made out the weekly shopping list she included 'bread for humans', 'bread for birds'. Winters in Montreal can be severe indeed and, but for a little thought on the part of humans, these creatures would stand little chance of survival during the long spells of frost and snow.

Yes, the time came when we would once more be moving further afield — and when we approached Mr. Gobeille to tell him of our plans, he would have been happy if he could have induced us to change our minds.

Some people imagine that after a person has written a book the author is owned by the public and he should be available at any time of the day or night. If they would only stop to think, writers need more peace and quiet than the so- called 'average' person because a good part of their time is spent in another dimension; they have to think and plan before they can write.

I am inclined to agree with the American writer, Scott Fitzgerald, who has been quoted as saying that 'Authors are many different people if they are any good at all at their craft.' This being so or not, peace and privacy are essential for an author to continue with his work. The Guv had completed two more volumes in spite of the many diversions and interruptions from would be well-wishers and curiosity seekers; but there was no other alternative to looking around for a more peaceful abode.

FLIGHT OF THE PUSSYWILLOW

CHAPTER TWENTY-THREE

When we had finally decided we would leave Montreal, and Habitat, I proposed that we might consider Alberta, the province of the Wild Rose; Calgary for choice. But it seemed the Dogwood of British Columbia beckoned more strongly.

It was my first visit to Vancouver and I must say that there is no exaggeration in the reports one is given as to its beauty; and the awesome grandeur of the Rockies is a sight all should see. We arrived on a hot July day, near the peak of the tourist season, and it seemed like another world compared to the Canada we had left behind. Where else could one find a modern cosmopolitan city, with the sea so close at hand, and yet in a few minutes find one's self in the midst of a setting such as can be found in an English countryside — the noted Stanley Park for instance.

It was in Vancouver that we accumulated a fair number of flowers and plants, providing an interest which I have maintained right up to the present. The Japanese bonsai tree is available in British Columbia and we had the good fortune to find one or two beautiful specimens of an advanced age — which made them even more desirable.

Then there was the terrarium where we had a glass container full of tiny plants and covered with a glass top which, if kept covered, is never (or very rarely) in need of water since by condensation it maintains its own level of humidity. Some people prefer colored glass for the container, but it is better for the plants if one uses a plain clear glass which allows the maximum amount of light to reach them since, without sufficient light, no plant will survive. I was interested to learn that it was a London surgeon, a stu- dent of natural history, who realized the possibilities of a terrarium and was able to send various grasses and ferns as far away as Sydney, Australia — a journey of eight months in those days, where they arrived in perfect condition. Successfully, this man was able to grow over one hundred specimens of fern and different grasses by the terrarium method, things considered impossible to grow in the polluted, sooty air of nineteenth-century London. So, almost one hundred and fifty years later, we can still give thanks to Dr. Nathaniel Ward for his wonderful discovery which brings so much joy into our present-day homes.

It is fortunate that the weather is mainly warm in Vancouver for a large percentage of the population consists of elderly, even old, people, many of whom are pensioners and who have a very limited income; so they do not need expensive winter clothing or need to spend too much on heating their homes. One day, while I was in a bakery shop, an elderly lady came in and asked the price of a cake; but apparently it was too expensive so she left, and it made me feel sad. The assistant commented, 'I see you were sorry for her — but you get used to it ' I was given to understand that it was never wise to buy anything for one of these people, however sorry you might feel. 'They are very proud, you know,' the assistant went on, 'and they are extremely independent.'

Twice I had an opportunity to take a trip to Vancouver Island, and I found the capital, Victoria, most interesting and quite British. To my regret there was no time to visit the famous Butchart's Gardens. The climate of course is much drier than the mainland and we had hopes of transferring ourselves over there. However, as I mentioned before, no one seemed interested in having Cat People, otherwise there would have been no problem; so, on each of my trips I went home disappointed.

One feels that the Rockies separate B.C. from the rest of Canada, in more ways than just physically, for the residents do not readily accept strangers. One gains much information about a place by listening to and observing taxi drivers — and Vancouver was no exception. We understood from them that to be a native of British Columbia was the ultimate achievement; and we learned much more. It was not possible to make a 'time call'; that is, arrange for a cab for a certain hour. I was quite concerned when I spent a day there last year and I tried to book a taxi to take me back to the airport. 'No Ma'am,' I was told, 'we cannot book anything in advance.' Nowhere else have I experienced this kind of attitude, so I was thankful to get back to Calgary where one can not only make previous arrangements but it is possible to ask for a certain driver. This is particularly helpful when a disabled person, such as the Guv, needs to make a journey.

And here the drivers do not change shifts in the middle of the afternoon, causing one to start out with one person and more than likely find it's three thirty and changeover time halfway through the outing. This happened to us several times; and I remember one day in particular when, just after lunch, I went with the Guv to West Vancouver where we had to do some shopping. It was a beautiful day so we drove along Ambleside Drive, enjoying the sea air; and when the time came to return it was the start of the rush hour. As everybody who lives in that area knows, you should never be in a hurry if you are crossing the Lion's Gate Bridge.

Well, there we were, stuck about halfway across in a real traffic jam, when over the radio came the voice of the dispatcher with a message for our driver: 'Come on, you'd better get going and check in — your night driver is waiting.'

The man was not in a very good mood so his reply was anything but pleasant. And there was nothing we could do except to exercise patience. Another time we actually did have the drivers change over their shifts — right in the center of Vancouver.

Our apartment was situated on a corner and the windows were large so there was plenty to see from each angle, especially in the direction of English Bay where sea-going vessels awaited their turn before entering the harbor. There was one day in particular that we spent a very enjoyable time watching kites being flown in the bay. These were man-lifting kites, and we enjoyed the display so much that it was impossible to get anything done in our household. One's mind went back to 'The Third Eye' and the description of these displays about which the Guv wrote.

Another window provided a view of the North, and some- times as I gazed down towards the Bayshore Inn I used to wonder how that well-known figure, Howard Hughes, was spending his time, where he occupied the top floor of the Bayshore. He had arrived in Vancouver just before we did; something of a mystery figure who reportedly only left his quarters except when traveling, although no doubt the art of disguise was quite familiar to him. I sometimes felt that we had something in common with Mr. Hughes in that a good deal of trouble had come our way, not of our own making.

Eventually, due to several reasons, it was necessary to cast around again for a peaceful place to settle down; and that was how we came to reconsider

FLIGHT OF THE PUSSYWILLOW

Calgary. Since no one in our Family had paid a visit to the up and coming city, it was decided someone should go; and this time it was my turn. It was around this time of the year, or a little earlier (March), when snow was still well in evidence; but I enjoyed the trip and was fortunate in meeting a person in the rental business, particularly apartments. Actually the person I met was the wife, and she freely offered helpful information, at the same time showing me an apartment in the building where she and her husband lived. This was one of the times when, apparently by chance, I just happened to meet the right people at the right time. And I found the experience quite agreeable after the negative attitude I had been experiencing with the Vancouver landlords.

Downtown Calgary may not be a place of beauty but when one looks out on the gray concrete buildings one can change the focus of one's eyes, looking further afield to the clear skies, and in the distance the foothills and the Rockies.

To make up for the lack of beautiful scenery the people are extremely friendly and helpful. And if one is prepared to drive about eighty miles along the expressway, there is nothing more beautiful than Banff (in the foothills and the lovely Lake Louise.

It was a few months before everything was finally arranged, while in the interval we basked in the sun of British Columbia; and a short time before we were due to leave the Guv had quite a bad period, due to a fall, which left us wondering however we would manage even a short journey, let alone the long trek to Alberta.

It was most upsetting for all of us — the Guv not being able to move because of pain in his back; and I felt quite helpless. The doctor came to visit; he was a nice man but there seemed nothing he could do either except to give a sedative with the hope that it would ease the pain (to be left lying on the bedroom floor for two or three days is not a happy experience because floors can be very hard over the carpet-covered concrete). One begins to think that if the physician is 'stumped' about what to do there is not much hope for the patient, and this was our position. One day he came in, chatted for a while, and then asked, 'Have you ever had this before?' When the Guv said he had, the doctor answered, 'Well, you've got it again!'

Vancouver seems to be a real refuge for the elderly and one can only conclude the attraction must be the more temperate climate, the less severe winters than is experienced by the remainder of the country. In the West End area it was most noticeable; you would see senior citizens on the bus and walking along the streets to the numerous stores, or wandering the short distance to enjoy the peace and beauty of Stanley Park. The number of wheel chairs around was greater than I had seen anywhere, apart from the Star and Garter Home for the war disabled — near Richmond Park, in Surrey, England.

The mall in Denman Street, at the corner of Comox, was very convenient for wheel chair passengers in that they were able to meet their friends and shop without suffering from the dampness or rain (of which Vancouver has an abundance) of the street outside. One could get a prescription and post one's letters at the same time in the drugstore cum post office, or do some food shopping in the supermarket across the way, and buy other things from shoes and clothing to delicate articles from the Chinese gift shop. Several elderly people moved into the apartments over the mall for this very reason — that shopping was less of a chore than having to carry supplies a few blocks away. It was obvious that, rather than a chore, buying supplies became quite a pleasure.

The older we become the more interested we are in the subject of age, and what comes after this life; for dying is a process which each of us must experience sooner or later. I have sometimes thought that being born should be of greater concern since this entails leaving our Home and going out into the unknown, to an unexplored strange place, that our progress may be hastened through the trials and tribulations we will surely encounter, and then — Home again. In many cases it is not growing old and dying which is the problem, but the real concern is often whether there will be anyone to care for us should we cease to be able to look after ourselves, and whether we will be able to manage from the financial aspect. When two people have spent the greater part of their lives together and one partner is left to face the loneliness — that is hard; and I know of one charming old gentleman who is in just that position. His health is very poor, as one might expect of a person well into his eighties, and while he is patiently living out his lifespan he will be happiest when the day comes when he will finally join his partner who he always refers to as 'my dear wife'.

There comes to mind the picture of two delightful people who I have met recently, and though they would be classed as elderly they are extremely energetic and mentally stimulating. I will call them Grandpa Reginald and

FLIGHT OF THE PUSSYWILLOW

Grandma Janet, and they arrived here from England just a few years ago. They are the grandparents of Andrew, who I mentioned before — the young man who decided the Guv was legless, and although we have had the pleasure of meeting them only once we have had many interesting conversations by telephone. Grandma has a wonderful sense of humor and she has many interesting experiences to relate, while Grandpa is quieter in manner, which is just as well since Grandma is lively enough for two. It just goes to show that age is not necessarily the gateway to misery.

CHAPTER TWENTY-FOUR

IT was early September when we came to Calgary, and we never expected we would be able to make the trip since the Guv continued to have a lot of pain and discomfort. However, as always, once he has made a decision, he always seems to be able to see it through, pain or no pain. It was nice to know too that Miss Cleo and Miss Taddy were welcome here, with no likelihood of suddenly being turned out of their home, because that meant one less worry for the Guv. In Vancouver, however, where the situation continued to deteriorate, pets and children were being turned away from the West End. We heard of a cat whose family had been asked to have 'Freddie' removed from the building immediately, otherwise notice would be given. And this was not an isolated case. Freddie was a mature Cat Person, of five years who had lived in apartments the greater part of his life, and he was a well-behaved responsible person. I did not hear the sequel to Freddie's plight but I certainly was thankful to get away from a situation such as this, which I understand is becoming more and more common.

Sometimes one feels one would like to own one's home where there would be no landlord to answer to, where one could do as one pleased. But it seems this is not to be; and, after all, there are many advantages to our present life style.

Here, our Cat Persons are treated very well, with the respect which is their due. I believe we are quite reasonable tenants, who do not cause too much trouble, and I like to think that Carol (who is in charge of this complex) would agree with this opinion. Perhaps I should ask her! I have several reasons for being interested in Carol, not the least of which is that she is amusing — of a type who prevents us all from getting too stuffy. Also, she is interested in things meta- physical, and I would say she is quite psychic; though, being modest, she would probably say, 'No, no, I just have a hunch about something occasionally.' Irish modesty no doubt! Did I say 'of a type'? Carol is unique. She very closely resembles my friend Suzzanne; and many of her 'mannerisms' are similar. The people we meet from day to day are very important in our lives for we often see more of them than we do of our relatives and close friends.

David Niven is another interesting personality, and this gentleman owns several jewelry stores. Actually his name is not Niven at all, but he resembles the actor and I happened to comment upon it one day, so the name has stuck. Whenever I telephone him he always answers, 'Hello, this is David Niven speaking! What can I do for you?' His wife is a most sympathetic and understanding person and she is a very interested reader of the Lobsang Rampa books, with a sincere belief in the author's concepts. It was indirectly through the Niven's that I visited the funeral home last Christmas. Mrs. M., whose husband had passed away, has been a member of the Niven's staff for many, many years.

Calgary is not so big that everybody becomes impersonal; thus it is that one is able to make worthwhile and lasting associations.

Our postal workers in the local office take a personal interest in helping their customers; and at present, while the country is in the throes of a rotating strike, the workers here find it most embarrassing, and they heartily dislike these disruptions.

There has been a lot of time for thinking since we came to Calgary, and the past few months has been a period of 'reviewing', of looking back to some extent to compare Yesterday with Today, considering how one might improve one's self in preparation for the tomorrows which all too soon will be Todays.

As one grows older one realizes the futility of such states as worry, fear, anger and the like; and the Guv has an expression for those who periodically give way to these emotions. He says, 'Why worry, it won't matter in fifty years time.' Quite a consoling thought. And there is an old saying which has much the same meaning:

'If there's a cure, try and find it

If there isn't, never mind it.'

I have learnt a great deal through my association with Lobsang Rampa, probably more than I will ever realize while I am on the earth. I would have

FLIGHT OF THE PUSSYWILLOW

to be pretty dim not to have benefited from the two decades of our association. I suppose the outstanding things which are likely to stay in my consciousness are:

(1) To mind one's own business and to keep one's counsel, not discussing other people's affairs to their detriment. Not to talk too much and not to tell everything you know. I have tried to follow this advice and sometimes it has been a great strain to refrain from saying, 'Oh I know about that; I will tell you.' But then I kept my counsel and I really find it interesting — to observe but to say nothing can be fun. People don't know how much you know and so they will tell you even more.

The Guv says that if you tell all you know, the other person will think you know even more, and then you have to work harder not to disappoint him.

I am reminded of one case in particular where a man talked too much of other people's affairs. He had recently become the manager of a bank and apparently he discussed the accounts of one person with another. When it became known what was happening (after someone complained), well, the poor man was demoted. No, this did not happen in Canada.

(2) TO BE CHARITABLE. . . . Next to minding one's own business, the giving of one's time, one's understanding, one's forgiveness, can bring joy to the recipient and contentment to the giver. Even one's material goods.

If we have two of something, why not give one to some- one who is without — if he can use it? Many people have commented upon the Guv's extreme kindness in this respect and I will go so far as to say that, if he had only one of something and another person needed it he would pass it on to the other person.

Unlike many of us, he does not give away only the things for which he has no use. He gives that which he treasures if he sees someone wants it.

It is his belief, and mine too, that if a person desires one of your possessions, that person puts his 'impression' on it, so in a way you have lost it; and the only thing to do is to hand it over; otherwise, every time you look upon it you will sense (unless you 'see' as the Guv does) the would be owner's 'impression' and you will no longer enjoy that particular possession. So why have two dis- satisfied persons? Better to give it away.

(3) TO DISCIPLINE ONE'S SELF. . . The difference between rabble and a well controlled army is just a matter of discipline. Anyone possessed of av-

erage intelligence knows that training and reliability make a better person.

Training consists merely of repetition, habit, or whatever we like to call it; and the first thing is to make a decision and stick to it. I have not met anyone who had so disciplined himself as Lobsang Rampa. He will never allow his physical to overcome his mental state; and the more desperately sick he may feel he will get up from his bed to prove to himself that his 'will' is the master of his body.

When I started to write these pages I felt the need to do something different and to work on it regularly, and I have found the discipline involved very beneficial. When I told Mr. Sowter I found writing very good therapy, he expressed surprise. He must have thought I was badly in need of therapy to adopt such stern measures.

(4) TO STAND ALONE. . . This, to many people, is probably the most difficult of all for, though we may have an independent nature, we do not like the idea of standing alone. The Guv has repeated over and over again that 'everyone must learn to stand on their own feet for it is the only way to progress'.

In the final analysis, NO ONE can escape; each one of us must account for himself. When on occasion I may have bemoaned the fact that life can be very lonely, I am told: 'You don't know what loneliness is until you go away from your own people and your own land, with no hope of returning: How would you like to be mis-understood and maligned when all you were trying to do was to help poor struggling humanity?'

I have thought about it and decided that I could not bear that kind of loneliness. In my saner moments I realize that, after all, compared to the Guv my conception of aloneness is nonexistent.

A Final Note

THIS morning I received a letter from a person who had been reading the Guv's latest book 'Twilight', and the writer suggested it would be nice if I were to write a book of my own. Apparently she liked my modest contribution to 'Twilight'.

So, to this reader and the many others who, through the years, have asked, 'Why doesn't Ra-ab tell HER story', I want you to know I appreciate your interest and I say, with Mrs. Fifi Greywhiskers, I do hope you will like my book.

FLIGHT OF THE PUSSYWILLOW

Thelma says she has enjoyed working on it, but I am sure she is relieved that we have finished the typescript; though, without her help I am sure it would have taken much longer to complete. I also wish to express my gratitude to Irene Clevering who allowed the work to be done, since she does not normally undertake literary material.

Let me finish with a tribute to cats and cat lovers, by the publisher of Cats Magazine, quoted from a Detroit News Story on cats, and reprinted in the April issue of the magazine: *'Cat lovers seem to be more sure of themselves and more satisfied with the way life is. They are less materialistic, and more thoughtful and kind.'*

THE END

www.ingramcontent.com/pod-product-compliance
Lightning Source LLC
Chambersburg PA
CBHW080533090426
42733CB00015B/2571